Spirits...
They Are Present

Janet Mayer

authorHOUSE®

AuthorHouse™
1663 Liberty Drive
Bloomington, IN 47403
www.authorhouse.com
Phone: 1-800-839-8640

First published by AuthorHouse 7/20/2011

ISBN: 978-1-4567-4377-2 (sc)
ISBN: 978-1-4567-4376-5 (hc)
ISBN: 978-1-4567-5178-4 (e)

Library of Congress Control Number: 2011903558

Printed in the United States of America

This book is printed on acid-free paper.

Cover illustrated by M.G.Brielmaier, oil on canvas, 11x14

Mom

My Hero
My Blessing

Contents

Prologue

*Taking a deep breath in.......... holding it.......... breathing
out. Evocative music vibrating through the room.*

As I lay on my blanket I hear others rustling around me. Laughter drifts
near. The music washes over me as I enjoy the peaceful stimulating feeling it
creates. Suddenly, across the room I hear a piercing scream. My peacefulness
is infiltrated with noises of pain and sorrow that send disturbing emotions
vibrating through me. I feel their cry of anguish and lay there, wondering,
"Am I doing the right thing by being here? Will this give me the answers I've
been searching for throughout my life?" Confused, I didn't really know, but I
wanted to take that chance and find out. I needed understanding. I needed
answers now! I could no longer coexist with the life I was leading and the
visions I was seeing. Visions I had no control over—visions I couldn't touch,
but nonetheless caused so much pain and suffering. I wanted understanding,
I wanted peace. I wanted control.

I heard an encouraging voice whisper with conviction in my ear, "Get up
and go to the bathroom." I acted on command. Slowly I silently moved through
the people who laid spread throughout the room and walked into the restroom.
I looked in the mirror as I washed my hands and wondered, "What's going
on, who spoke to me?" I calmly walked back into the room and once again
laid down upon my blanket when beyond my control something inconceivable
happened. Out of nowhere words began pouring out of me. Phraseology that
I had never heard before, "Sa-la-may-pay, sa-la-may-pay," gaining force it

shuttered through my chest and up my neck straining my vocal cords with a massive energy behind it. SA-LA-MAY-PAY, I continued speaking, as it swiftly rolled off my tongue. The pressure in my chest was overwhelming yet for some reason I never feared I couldn't hold the energy rumbling through my body. My tongue felt like it was twisted and stretched moving in a way that offered no explanation to what was happening. A language was emerging. Forty-five minutes rolled by and yet it felt like only seconds. The feeling that came with this language was euphoric. I just wanted to stay within it and feel, yet I had to let go as it began to slip away and then vanish. As I slowly became aware of my surroundings, I realized the session was over and I opened my eyes. Everyone in the room was staring at me. What in the hell just happened? Didn't I have enough on my plate already?

This book is my incredible journey through life and where it has led me so far. I've traveled through twists and turns I could have only wished were in a book of fiction.

I've walked a path most would have never thought "possible," a path I was fearful of as a child, didn't want to know about as a teenager, and now as an adult, want answers I can't live without. So come join me on this path, walk with me, hold this book as if you're holding my hand. See the journey I live day by day, from the fears, to the pain, and to all the many discoveries made along the way which brought healing to myself and others.

PART I

The Beginning

Chapter One

The Visions

To climb steep hills requires slow pace at first.
William Shakespeare

At age five I was like any little kid on the block. I watched cartoons, had tea parties with my stuffed animals, played with dolls, did somersaults under the sweet gum tree and tried to do anything my older sisters did, unless it included dirt or being barefoot. After all, the one time I ran around in the grass without my shoes on enjoying the texture of the summer blades, I stepped on a bee. It stung me right between the toes and that was the end of going barefoot.

Yet one night, my life was irreversibly changed forever. I awoke startled in the middle of the night to see my dad leaning against the door frame of the entrance to my bedroom. This normally wasn't anything extraordinary since Mom and even Dad tucked my sisters and I in every night. However this night was quite different. I had already been tucked in hours beforehand. Now my dad was once again standing in the doorway and I could literally see *through* him. His complete form took up most of the doorway and yet I could see the prayer of St. Francis of Assisi that hung on the wall behind him, as well as the harvest gold phone next to it. I *knew* that this wasn't right and yet couldn't understand how I could so clearly see the side of his face and print of his pajamas, yet see past him. My five year old mind had a tough time solving this illusion before me. How can someone look transparent and yet opaque? I must have made a sound because he suddenly shifted. He lifted his head from where it was resting on his arms against the doorframe and looked right at me. I saw his face and glanced up to his eyes. The power of his stare was so intense, I screamed. Fear turned my vocal cords so tight that I wondered if I woke up half of the neighborhood. My mom came sprinting down the hall, right through my dad and into the bedroom stopping in front of my bed, insisting, "What's wrong?" I was so frightened that I could hardly speak, except to say, "I saw a ghost and it was dad. He, he, he...... disappeared when you ran through him." I began to look around the room and into all the shadowed dark corners. *Where did he go?* Mom, not knowing the extent of my nighttime visitor assumed I had a bad dream. She sat on the bed beside me and began to rub my back to calm me down. Her comfort and presence was essential. It took a long time that night for my breathing to get back to a more normal pace and before I finally fell back to sleep praying I wouldn't wake until the morning light.

After that, I became very frightened at night, always checking under the bed before I jumped in. Looking in the closet to make sure no one was hiding in there, I wouldn't go to bed until a night light was on, hoping that would keep the ghost away. I wasn't afraid of my dad but I was worried about him turning into a ghost each night. Would it happen again? I slept with the covers to my nose and my stuffed pink dog beside me to hide from any ghost that may be lurking in the hidden corners of my room. By the time I realized my dad had actually been astral traveling all those many years ago, I had moved on toward substantially more alarming and scarier things.

It was Christmas Day. Being a young adult I was considerably excited about the day that was before me—Church, presents, seeing the family and having a party, I couldn't wait. It was the best day of the year as far as I was concerned. My family and I first went to visit my grandmother Helen who was in a nursing home. She suffered a stroke years earlier and needed physical therapy on a daily basis so this home was the perfect fit for her. We walked in her room and as I was standing in front of her, I suddenly knew this would be the last time I would see her. I had no idea where that thought came from, but it hit me like a flash of lightning. I gazed into her eyes and as she looked at me, I almost felt like she was saying goodbye. As if we had a secret message between us somehow. There were no words, only a knowing beyond my understanding at that time. I didn't know how to react. Sadness, shock and a peaceful feeling embraced me as well. I was too afraid to say anything. How do you tell your parents that you think Grandma is going to die today, but it's okay? At my age they would have thought I was crazy—After all, *I thought maybe I was crazy. Where did that thought come from? Why would I even think that? What kind of granddaughter am I?*

Later that night the nursing home called to tell us Grandma had passed in her sleep. I couldn't believe it, but I knew it was true. I knew things I didn't want to know. More importantly, I was afraid I made it happen and that's what really scared me.

So I tried to push this knowing aside and did a really good job for a while, or so I thought until my other Grandma, Eleanor, died around the following Easter. She appeared to me the following night and flowery stencils of "E's and F's" appeared all over my wall as if she produced them with a magic wave of her hand. It was nice at first, because her initials gave me a peaceful feeling. Interestingly she didn't say anything. She smiled and looked so wonderful and even younger than I remembered. It just reminded me of all the times we went to her house on Sundays for dinner with our cousins. She left me with a warm and comforting feeling, until she disappeared, when abruptly I was once again scared, and back to having a night light on. *I was afraid if Grandma Eleanor could visit then who next? Maybe somebody I didn't know? Maybe somebody who looked scary or was a criminal! Could they possibly hurt me? If they appeared, what else could they do that I didn't know of? Could they maybe touch me?* My mind began to conjure up images of all sorts of scary scenarios. It freaked me out to think that at any time someone might just appear and I couldn't stop that from happening. I admit I'm a chicken. Miss Janet Chicken. So again, I tried to block all this out. I didn't have anyone to tell me what to do, so I let my thoughts rule my actions. And my thoughts were the fear of the unknown. Would time change my perspective and take away the apprehension I lived with? It was an unquestionable, no.

As I grew into my teenage years I realized I had several abilities emerging that were fun for a girl my age, enough so that it became noticeable to those around me. Not realizing this at the time, I often received random bits of intuition taking place when I was relaxed and focused on the mundane. It was a sunny Saturday morning and I was sitting at the kitchen table doing homework. Suddenly, I heard the phone ringing in my head and as a reflex, I yelled, "Phone!" seconds before it actually rang expecting someone else to get it since I was busy. I was somewhat startled by the noise when it did ring because I wasn't really paying attention to the outside world or even thinking about what I said until after the fact. I didn't know who was calling, nor did I care. I was more amazed that I knew it was going to happen and the fact that I heard it in my mind before it took place. I remember sitting at the table looking out the window over the rooftops wondering, "Could I do that again?"

Sometimes I saw flashes of pictures in my mind and then that scenario would be played out at a later date. I once saw a vision of my cousin getting a new car, and later that same day she called saying, "Hey guess what Janet?" I knew the color too. Of course, that wasn't the only way I received information.

My high school required all students to take a hearing exam as part of state requirements. That was fine by me since I would be getting out of class work. Standing in line to get a hearing test and chatting with my girlfriends made anything required by the state acceptable. It was my turn to sit and take the basic raise-your-hand-when-you-hear-the-beep test. This was going to be a cinch. After completing the exam, the nurse, Ann, looked at me with concern. She handed me the results, saying, "You need to take a more in-depth assessment." What? I failed the hearing exam? Then Ann gave me instructions on where to go and a form to fill out. Mom made the appointment and the following week we arrived for my second hearing test. The technician ushered me into a square room that looked like a bank vault with padded dark green walls. There was only a single chair in the middle of the room and a set of headphones. The lighting left a faint shadowy glow leaving the room even less desirous. One wall held a window and on the opposite side was the technician and all of her screening equipment. Although feeling apprehensive, I put on the headset. "Raise your right or left hand when you hear the beep in that ear," she instructed. Okay, that sounded simple to me. Then again, I thought it was simple last time, and look what happened. I heard the beep and raised my right hand. The technician said, "I haven't pressed the button, yet." So we tried again. Feeling nervous now, *I better pay closer attention.* Once again, I heard the beep and raised my right hand. "I haven't pressed the button yet!" the technician complained. I sat there and waited, *maybe I was supposed to wait for two beeps? I'll just wait.* When I heard the first beep and then a second stronger one, I raised my hand. Finally I was doing it correctly. I passed the test. As we were walking down the hall toward my mom, I apologized, "I'm sorry I wasn't waiting for the second beep." "There weren't two beeps—only one at a time," the technician replied. I glanced up at her, dumbfounded. I wasn't going to argue with her since I had just completed the test and passed. We met my mom and the technician told her, "We had a little difficulty at the beginning, but then Janet did just fine. She kept raising her hand before I touched the button, but I'm sure that was just a coincidence." I left there confused. I didn't know what to think, and I believe the technician felt the same way. I realized later that I was actually hearing the beeps before they sounded. How cool was that? And yet, how did I do that? Did it just take a quiet sound proof room to make me realize all I had to do was focus? Could it be that simple? Maybe I needed to pay more attention and see what else I could do.

My sister, Debbie, was one of the first to notice my abilities. While she was at work, I called to chat and during our conversation, in my mind I began to see pink squares all over her office. It was distracting. I thought, *"What the heck is she doing?"* So I asked. "Debbie, I keep seeing flashes of pink squares all over your office." She laughed, informing me, "I do have millions of pink Post-it squares all over my office walls, furniture and anything that moves. I'm moving into a different office and the Post-it notes tell the movers where everything is supposed to be placed in the new office." After that, I closed my eyes and scanned around her office in my mind and stopped at her desk and asked, "Did you by any chance have chocolate chip cookies and popcorn for lunch today?" "Yes, and I hate it when you do that Janet," she replied laughing, along with me. I caught her eating junk food again! Debbie soon became an instrument for me, a compass to help guide me on my future path.

Beyond noticing my abilities, Debbie was curious. Prior to a business trip to Germany, she asked, "Can you tell me if you see anything around the plane? Is it safe to fly?" Because she asked, I sat down to see if I could get anything and why not, this could be interesting. So, I started off by meditating or what I thought would be meditating. Having no prior knowledge I was making it up as I went along. I just sat in a chair and got comfortable, closed my eyes and had a pen and paper ready in case anything emerged that I would need to remember. I said a little prayer thinking that was the "right" thing to do and waited. I tried to remain quiet and calm and breathed in and out slowly while odd bits and pieces of random information would flutter through my mind. I pushed past it and asked the question, "Is Debbie's flight to Germany safe?" Sure enough that quick, a vision appeared right in front of my closed eyes. I saw the airplane taking off and landing safely in a matter of seconds. I then started to have an uncomfortable feeling, something didn't feel right. I tried to force myself to see something but nothing came. So I sat and relaxed once again focusing on the feeling and nothing else. There is a problem, a small problem, but not in the engine. I couldn't see exactly what it was, however I somehow knew she wasn't in any danger yet something wasn't quite right. I told her what I got and she wrote it down. After landing, she immediately called me from Germany. "There was in fact a problem on the plane, Debbie explained. It was the lavatory. The one closest to her didn't work properly. Shortly after takeoff the flight attendant announced, 'Everybody must use the lavatory in the back of the plane.' It wasn't a safety issue, but on such a long flight, it was an inconvenience."

By my late teens and early twenties my abilities began to amplify in many directions. Thinking I was doing a good thing and out of kindness, I decided to warn my new boyfriend that weird things happened around me and I seemed to know random bits of information about what seemed like unimportant things. I also let him know that I often knew about some events before they happened. I didn't want to tell him too much and scare him away, but I just wanted to prepare him in case. "I don't believe any of that hocus pocus crap," Carl said, "You can believe that stuff if you want to, but don't tell me about it because you'll be wasting your breath. It's ridiculous." Great start, right? Good thing I was used to some skepticism from those around me, so why not him too? Unfortunately for him it didn't take long before he saw what I was talking about.

After a late dinner and movie in the city, Carl was driving me home. It was about a twenty minute drive. I dozed off due to an exhausting day at work and a fun filled evening, when suddenly awake, I blurted out, "Oh no! There's an accident up ahead over that hill." I rambled, "I see a helicopter, and a body with a sheet over it on the highway, and police cars everywhere." Carl looked over at me as if I grew a second head and stated, "You fell asleep and must have been dreaming." I just sat there looking at him. I knew what I saw, and it wasn't a dream, it was real. The vision woke me up and made me feel like I was standing in the middle of it all. I sat impatiently and waited, knowing what I was about to see up ahead. Nervous at this point, I wasn't about to add any more information to Mr. He-Who-Doesn't-Believe. What was the point?

As we crested the hill a horrid nightmare was laid out before us. On the other side of the highway, police cars were all around, a helicopter had landed on the middle of the highway, and a body with a sheet over it was laid out for all to see. Cars were twisted and molded into disturbing shapes. I thought I was going to be sick right then and there but I couldn't look away. It was a mirror image of my vision. Carl just looked at it and kept driving. Neither of us spoke. Moments passed, and I glanced over to see his white knuckles poking out of his hands and what looked like a death grip holding on the steering wheel. He quietly spoke and then with volume, "How did you know? How could you have described that in such detail? You were sleeping!" I then took the time to carefully explain and to remind him that I see things. Sometimes while sleeping, sometimes while awake. I may get a quick flash or a sudden "knowing." I don't know how I know what I do, it just is. That night long ago was a wake up call for Carl and a reminder to me that once again I saw things I didn't wish to see. I can no longer try to ignore what exists.

Although there were many unpleasant visions, I also experienced many other types of interesting phenomena. A couple of playful visitors in my bedroom made sure of that even though I couldn't see them, they let me know they existed. Coming home from work each day, my first priority was get to the bedroom and slip off my work shoes placing them near the mirrored closet doors as usual. Of course being the anal person that I am, they had to be placed next to each other, but not touching. I admit I can be a pain in the ass at times. If you were to walk in my bedroom I would know it. Not one thing could be out of place. I'm a neat freak and crave organization.

Following routine, I headed to the kitchen for a bite to eat. When finished, I headed back to the bedroom to change into something more comfortable. It was then I noticed my shoes were disturbed. The left one was sideways instead of straight. *I didn't do that, did I?* Not thinking too much about it, I moved the shoe back into place. Must have been in a hurry, but that was certainly odd I told myself. It only took a couple of days to realize something was going on, something very strange. Amazingly my shoes would move daily, often two or three times. I told no one at first, in fear that my family might think I was crazy. After about a month, it was time to let others in on my discovery since it continued to happen. That's when I finally told my Mom as well as my boyfriend, Carl, about this interesting occurrence. I asked them to peek in my room and check out the shoes and their placement. Mom and Carl walked into my room and saw where the shoes were placed in front of the mirrored closet doors. Coming out into the family room Carl asked me, "What's this about? Why did you want us to look at your shoes?" and I responded, "You'll see." A short time later I asked them to return to my bedroom and check out the shoes once again. They were amazed. The left shoe had moved. This happened repeatedly and always to the left shoe. We could walk in the other room and back, and it would happen. Everyone could leave the house and it would be moved when we returned. So what did this mean? Why was it happening? Was I making this happen? I didn't think so since it took me days to even realize it was happening. Oddly enough, it only happened in my room. It didn't bother me and often made me smile. This was pretty cool if you ask me. That was only the beginning.

Waking up one gloomy morning, I noticed my mirrored closet sliding doors were open. At first I thought I forgot to close them but checked that thought, I knew better. Was someone playing tricks on me? Trying not to let it bother me it did leave me feeling a bit eerie. My mom and brother were the only ones who could have done that. So I began to watch and stay up late. Night after night they would slide open while I slept. This began to bother me. It wasn't until a door slid open after I awoke in the middle of the night that I got totally freaked out. I jumped out of bed so fast I tripped on the covers and almost landed on my face. Turning on the light as I ran by and down the hall I stopped and listened. My heart was pounding out of my chest as I waited. I turned around and started to quietly walk back to my bedroom. *I'm losing it, I thought.* This was too much for me to take in and it was scaring the shit of out of me. Walking back into the room I looked around and nothing. The room was quiet and the door was cracked open, just like previous nights, only this time I saw it happen. I sat on my bed staring at the mirrored closet doors for what seemed like hours. My mind was listing off possibilities of what just happened. Coming to the only logical conclusion, besides the fact I was crazy, is that I realized I had a menacing ghost residing in my bedroom. My shoes moved, my closet door and even a couple things on my dresser seemed out of place. They never harmed me but I can't say I was happy about them being there either. I decided the next day to sit on my bed and ask these unseen entities to please stop. Being raised Catholic, I added a prayer for good measure thinking this was the thing to do. Besides, it couldn't hurt to say a couple of "Our Fathers" right? Hopefully they understood the message. I thanked them for their version of entertainment and assured them it was time to move on. Believe it or not, my roommates left. My room fell silent and still once more. No more moving shoes and the closet doors stayed shut. I think back to those days wondering if they came to offer me a reprieve from all the negative experiences that I was consuming. *Did they tease to make me smile? Or were they testing me for the future?* Watching shoes move was exciting, but the sliding doors opening gave me the feeling of an intruder. That was extremely unsettling to think about. I constantly wondered if someone was lurking behind in the deep recess of the darkened closet. Luckily, things settled down in my bedroom and everything was going to be just fine.

A few months later Carl was at my house celebrating New Year's Day with my family and I. Being Irish, we had great parties and the New Year was a perfect excuse to celebrate! It was an afternoon party that extended into the evening. Family members were leaving since they had to work the next day. However, as Carl was getting ready to leave I began to get this feeling around him and it wasn't a good one either. It was around 9:00 p.m. and I suddenly found myself begging him not to leave. I just had a horrible feeling coming from around him. I didn't want him driving home. I could see I was getting the message across when he asked, "What's wrong, what are you seeing?" I stated, "I'm having another one of my bad feelings, as I started to call them and it's connected around you in some way. I don't want you to leave yet. Please do not walk out that door, at least until the feeling has passed, okay?" as I held his hands tightly as if glued as one. "Alright, if it makes you feel better, I'll stay but just for a little while longer," Carl replied. And so we sat. For more than an hour we huddled together until that disturbing feeling I was carrying finally dissipated. In the past, when one of those unsettling feelings would come upon me, I'd find myself constantly pacing, not even being able to sit still for a moment. That night, I held Carl's hand, jumped up once or twice and then immediately sat back down to guard Carl in some mystical way. I remained near him to make sure he didn't decide to leave before my feeling did. As time slowly drifted, I began to feel the heavy weight lift. I turned to him and said, "Okay, the feeling is gone, whatever was going to happen, I think you're safe. When you get home, you call me." Carl hugged me, kissed me goodbye and out the door he went. He called as soon as he got home to let me know he made it safely.

Early the following morning my phone rang and I reached over to pick it up. My hello a bit groggy, Carl's voice was on the other end. By his tone I knew something was very wrong and sat up in bed. The news was heart-rendering. He called from work to inform me he just found out a friend and co-worker, whose locker was next to his, was in a car accident the night before and was killed on impact. It happened shortly after 9:00 pm. We cried. Tears of hopelessness rained down my face. Guilt seemed to eat away at my thoughts because I couldn't stop that from happening, that I thought it was Carl, not his friend who was going to be hurt and then I got extremely angry, at who, I didn't know—myself, God, the other driver. *Why in the hell couldn't I stop that from happening?* My mind was whirling. I had pieces, but not the complete puzzle. This man was young; he had his whole life ahead of him. *Why didn't I get more information? What use am I if I can't stop a tragedy I knew was going to happen?* This isn't a gift or ability, it is pure hell and I am forced to live it.

Chapter Two

Heaven & Hell

To conquer fear is the beginning of wisdom.
Bertrand Russell

By my mid-twenties I felt I was beginning to live through an odd semblance of heaven and hell. Vivid split-second visions seemingly came out of nowhere of people dying before they actually did flashed constantly through my mind. The only thing that made it worse was I couldn't stop any of it from happening. It was like living in a slow motion horror show. This was now a part of my life and dealing with it became one of my main priorities that I wasn't ready to face.

Despite my atypical life, I was now married to Carl. He began to watch vigilantly as my visions became reality, while I watched vigilantly as a skeptic became an advocate. Disturbed by what I saw, Carl became a constant source of comfort and often was a sounding board for my thoughts and worries. Our strong bond of love was vital, a fortress to retreat to when witnessing the path of death. Money, diamonds, a fancy car or a lovely home, can quickly bring comfort and happiness but not necessarily love or peace. My visions became stronger and although I had love, peace was left in the dust.

Striving to deal with my life, I was hoping that by applying the Zen philosophy of living in the moment, and enjoying the simple things, my visions would dissipate. It was my only plan. Best laid plans seem to have a habit of changing and this was no exception. Since my visions were coming at an erratic pace, I decided to search for answers and found some of them through many books. I was able to put a name to some of what I was experiencing and that pleased me. Being a very structured person, my visions never seemed to equate to the sum total of what I wanted these abilities to provide me with. Spiritual books definitely started me on the right track. I'm clairvoyant, clairaudient, clairsentient, with a bit of claircognizance, clairgustance and clairalience thrown in. All of them beginning with *clair* meaning "clear" and all are a form of extra sensory perception meaning information acquired from other than your physical senses. Clairvoyance is literally clear seeing, such as the images that flash in my mind. This means I can see almost anything under the right circumstances. What it doesn't mean is that I'll always understand what I'm seeing and it's not all black and white. A car accident can obviously be interpreted when it flashes in my mind but knowing who this happened to, to what extent, or why is another story. Clairaudience is clear hearing or listening in a paranormal way, through noises, tones, voices or even hearing a word but not the actual sound of it. This was experienced during my hearing test I spoke of in the last chapter, hearing the beep sounds before they happened. Also, Spirits have whispered messages to me that have stayed with me to this day. Clairsentience means clear feeling. A perfect example would be, not wanting Carl to leave the night of the party because of the way I felt. I didn't know exactly what was going to happen but it felt very menacing. I kept him near me until that feeling dissipated. This can also be related to anyone who speaks of having a gut feeling about someone or something. Claircognizance means clear knowing and it is my favorite. It's one thing to get a feeling, vision or hear something that no one else does, but to experience spontaneous knowledge and not know where it originates is powerful in a simplistic way. The last two are clairgustance which is the sense of taste without actually tasting anything and clairalience the same for clear smelling. An example of clairgustance would be when I had this sudden taste of cherries, almost as if just eating a whole bowl full and then I ran into a good friend, Phil, whose employer made cherry flavoring for an ice cream label. Clairailence could be explained by smelling something where this would not normally take place. I've encountered cigarette smoke when no one smokes around me, in a home where no smoking is allowed; also, I smelled perfume of a loved one who has previously passed years before. After reading about these different types of ESP I realized I've experienced all of them, a number of them at the same time. That's not to say I'm highly skilled in all of them, I just possess them and know they exist on some level. I was sort of Janet-of-all-trades, master-of-none at this point in my life. Yet unlike most of the books out there where mediums had all these wonderful adventures, I frankly could not say that. I couldn't relate with them because we weren't having the same scary experiences and if we were, they weren't writing about them. One piece of good advice I did learn was to take what "feels right" and leave the rest.

Although there was a feeling of moving forward in many areas of my life, it felt as if I was still going through heaven and hell. Being married was my heaven, such a wonderful new beginning in my life. I felt like a bright kite on a warm summer day, flying high above the earth floating back and forth with the soft winds. Then the visions would intrude upon my life as if the kite caught a strong wind and began to nosedive, slamming into the hard cold ground of reality. It was beginning to take its toll. I never knew what was going to happen next and I was often feeling drained as if waiting and worrying about the next vision that would emerge. How did it go from a ghost in the night as a child, to a total blowout of seeing dead people in my twenties? I didn't want this to be happening. Ok, so I found it extremely fascinating that this could be happening, but I didn't want to see most of what was being shown to me. Couldn't I just be shown the winning numbers to the lottery or something fun like that? It's not that simple, unfortunately. The anxiety the visions were causing made me fearful of starting a family. Working part time as a floral designer was a wonderful escape from some of those fears. Arranging bouquets of beautiful flowers knowing they will bring happiness to someone has always been a passion of mine that has brought pure enjoyment. Since family and only a handful of friends knew of my experiences, to the outside world my life was ordinary. This is how I wanted it. I had to find the answers on my own; besides, no one would want to know what I was seeing anyway. It never seemed favorable. I read any spiritual book I could get my hands on. "Think positive," became a mantra. Praying for answers seemed to be a constant focus. I was even trying to "turn it off" like a switch of the light as a number of books proclaimed could be done. Turn it on when I wanted to see something, turn it off when I didn't. So, how could this be done when no one showed you where the light switch was? Wandering around in the darkness searching for the light switch can often be quite a challenge, but I was up for it. Obviously something more was going on than was even imaginable from my limited perspective. The so called spirit world seemed to have a lot in store for me, and it looked as if this was going to be my mission in life. This would be Project Janet. Going into this apprehensively was putting it lightly to say the least, but I wasn't given much of a choice. Fearfully, I decided to plunge full throttle into the unknown committed to Project Janet.

I began to notice something that really amplified my awareness. I began to feel "Spirits" around me. It didn't matter what time of day or night, they would seem to just manifest an energy near me without warning, leaving me with subtle hints of suggestive knowledge. If you have ever had that feeling of someone behind you only to turn around and no one was there, it was that type of feeling only heavier, denser almost as if you could actually touch them, but not see them. So now instead of having a feeling, I would have a feeling that was accompanied by a "Spirit." Trends of seeing spirits before people passed left me with obvious realizations. They were around me. I tried to focus and pay extra attention to anything that felt out of the ordinary, but I was frightened. They weren't out to hurt me, I understood that much. It was almost as if they were teaching me as well as trying to warn me, even bring comfort beforehand, but I couldn't see it at the time. Besides, this wasn't exactly my form of comfort. Comfort for me is a toasty blanket and vanilla ice cream or maybe a fancy coffee, but not Spirits popping out of who knows where.

One evening, curled up on the couch relaxing, reading a juicy novel, totally engrossed in the characters and the deeply set plot, I began feeling the energy in the room subtlety change. As always, it was unexpected. Like a cold breeze, I began to feel a group of spirits gathering in my living room, and we're not talking about just a few. They filled the small space to capacity, like a crowded elevator. The longer I sat there, the more their presence was felt, expanding towards me, making me take note of the large gathering. In my head, I hear the phrases, "It's almost time, We have to hurry, Is everyone here?" and I could feel them moving about the room as if gliding about in slow motion and with extreme excitement I knew deep within they were preparing for a new arrival among them. The book slammed shut and I jumped up quickly and turned to Carl across the room. Chills running down my spine, I looked over to him and said, "We've gotta get outta here, now." I couldn't sit there for another minute; I had to get out of the house.

"Why?" Carl asked.

"Because I feel Spirits in every corner of this room and I think they are trying to tell me somebody is going to die tonight!"

"Ok, I'll get the car keys," he replied as he stood up.

I made Carl drive around to every family member's house I could think of, to make sure there wasn't an ambulance sitting in someone's driveway. This feeling was so overpowering and I felt so helpless. I *knew*, I experienced something extraordinarily surreal. They were preparing to greet someone and soon. Carl drove around until the feeling dissipated and I was somewhat calmed down.

Hours later, I was mentally exhausted when we returned home. I walked inside and although their presences were no longer there, the message they had given me left me frightened and physically, emotionally and spiritually drained. Now I had to wait for the big event that was about to take place: the death of a loved one. I never knew you could have hundreds of people packed into such a tiny space, but I can assure you Spirits do not take up much room.

The follow morning, I hate to say, I waited for a call. When the phone rang I stared at it like it grew two heads. Coffee cup in hand and not wanting to move I slowly reached over to grab the phone. I picked it up, answering it with tears in my voice. My mother-in-law was on the other end. She realized that I was crying and wanted to know what was wrong. I told her about the bad feeling I had the night before and tried to brush it off as a misunderstanding on my part. Two days later I was proven my original interpretation was correct. Al, a relative on my husband's side of the family died. Interestingly, the night the Spirits were gathering we had earlier went to dinner at a place right down the street from where Al lived. I was upset to find out the news, yet afterwards it helped when I recalled that he had one heck of a group of folks waiting for his arrival. We can only hope someday we'll all have a similar welcoming party. It was a scary lesson to learn, one that shook me up, but I did later see it as a blessing in disguise.

I found out quickly that Spirit had more lessons for me to learn. After getting ready for bed one night and snuggling under the covers, I leaned over to kiss Carl good night, but he was already sleeping so I turned back over on my right side. It wasn't more than a minute or two when I felt this gentle push against my left shoulder as if nudging me to roll over on my back. It was an odd sensation. I laid there wondering what that was about and how that could happen, when suddenly I was pushed harder and physically landed on my back. Before I could think, I opened my eyes and saw a woman standing at the end of my bed. She wasn't completely opaque, but somewhat translucent. Staring in awe and trying to take in what I was seeing, I first noticed she had what looked like a "Gibson girl" hair style. The face seemed to hide in shadows so I never quite saw the features looking back at me. Her clothes were white with a bluish tint and resembled a modern day sweat suit, except there was a broad wire-collared necklace that lay against her neck and on the blouse she wore. It reminded me of the necklaces you would see during the Egyptian era. It seemed to be there for a reason, not just for adornment. How I knew this, I don't know. The right arm and hand was extended out toward the window and the left arm was above her head with the hand tilted over and toward the window as well. My first thought was that she looked like an older woman standing in a dance position with arms poised. Complete quietness, I laid motionless staring at the scene before me. Suddenly, the most vibrant colors of neon lights I have ever experienced radiated from the woman's solar plexus' and came towards me, enfolding me in a rainbow of color. This tremendous electrifying energy, greater than any "earth love" I have experienced touched me. Imagine your greatest single moment when you experienced love, times that by a trillion and it still wouldn't equate to what I felt. It was powerful, all consuming, warm and gracious at the same time. If I could stay within that feeling forever, I would gladly do so. Suddenly she disappeared and the feeling went with her. The abrupt emptiness washed over me and snapped me back into reality. Holy shit, there was a woman at the end of the bed and I wasn't afraid. I smacked Carl to wake him up, "Honey, there was a woman at the end of our bed," and I started shaking him to wake him up. "Honey, wake up, there was a woman at the end of our bed." Carl groggily replied, "Yeah, Yeah, Ok, now go back to sleep." Here I am smacking him repeatedly and he is telling me to go back to sleep? Ok fine! But, there was a woman at the end of our bed!

The next morning as Carl got ready for work he wanted to know about the woman I was talking about when I woke him up the night before. I explained what I saw. He, like I, had no idea why she showed up or what it could mean. I joked that maybe it was just a feel good visit and then rolled over and decided to go back to sleep as Carl left for work. I jumped when the front door burst open nearly dislodging the hinges and Carl came flying up the stairs to the bedroom saying "Janet, I know why the woman came to you. Someone broke into our van last night and stole all my tools!"

"Are you serious?" I asked, thinking he was joking.

"Yes, I'm serious—they even left the door open." Then it hit me. The woman was actually pointing at the window. I felt like such an idiot—all I had to do was get up and look out the window. I guess I shouldn't have been so hard on myself, after all it's not every night someone appears as a translucent apparition to let you know someone is stealing from you. I couldn't fathom what she was trying to show me. Needless to say, another lesson learned, pay attention to everything that they show me, whether it's an arm, a leg or whatever. You just never know. I played charades with Spirit and lost, at least that was my thinking while filling out the insurance papers. What a hassle. Oh well, you live, you learn.

A couple of nights after that amazing visitation, and a pivotal moment in the history of Janet, I was about to encounter another life altering experience. The woman who had made her appearance was still in the forefront of my mind. Although I hadn't been afraid that night, afterwards I found myself peeping around corners before going into a room, leaving lots of lights on in the evening and sleeping with a night light. It can't be helped, as I mentioned earlier, I *am* sort of a chicken and what happened next proved it.

The rituals of putting my son to bed began as every night did. Matt was under a year old. First a diaper change and then I would dress him in a little one piece sleeper. I would lay him in his crib and sing to him and scratch his back. (This is back in the day when children were supposed to sleep on their stomachs). I sang the same three songs adding my own words to parts I didn't like from the originals. On this night after a busy day I was extremely tired and practically hanging over the crib, singing quietly, with my hand slowly scratching up and down his back. Up and down, slowly scratching with the rhythm of the song. Up and down, up and down, as the song came to an end, I commented out loud, "Matt honey, wish someone would scratch my back." And with that, someone did. I flew up so fast I almost fell over backward. Whipping around to find no one there but empty space, I walked out of the room shaking uncontrollably. Heart palpitations and shortness of breath, I was no longer tired and ended up waiting for Carl to get home. The lesson I learned that night? Be careful what you wish for, you just may get it.

***

Coincidentally or not, growing up I heard of a man, Edgar Cayce, who was known as the "Sleeping Prophet." He'd fall into a self-induced sleep state and answer questions about people and their lives: past, present and future. His insight ranged from health to love, along with anything else you wanted to know. His "readings" as they became known, are documented, and contain an astonishing amount of verifiable information. He was an amazing man who could see beyond the world we know by tapping into the "Akashic Records," as he called them, for answers. Edgar Cayce was a normal man by all standards, yet had an incredible ability and became an inspiration to many. He didn't have to be with a person to give them a reading—they could be thousands of miles away, but he was able to "tune" into the Akashic Records and provide answers to everyday life issues. Although I knew I wasn't anything like him, I was interested in his fascinating life, especially because I had so many unusual things happen around me. Maybe he had some answers from his life work that could possibly help me.

When I heard about a conference at the Association for Research and Enlightenment (A.R.E.) in Virginia Beach on psychic abilities and dreams based on Edgar Cayce's teachings, I jumped on it. My sister Debbie showed interest as well, so we signed up for one of the weekend courses and drove from Missouri to Virginia Beach, Virginia. As we arrived, nothing was more invigorating than breathing in the ocean air. We took the shuttle from our hotel to the A.R.E. headquarters and signed in for the weekend. This was a great step for me to take in my Spiritual transition. One of the experiments was focused on what we could see about the person sitting across from us. We were given exercises on relaxation and opening the mind. Never having met this person I sat across from, I closed my eyes and asked what I needed to see for her and then said: "Laura, you have a blue car."

"I do," she replied.

"You also have earthquakes around you, do you live in California?"

"Yes, I do."

I was so excited that I had actually received clear information, I lost my focus and couldn't get anything after that. Well, I was learning after all. It did make me realize we all have this capability to some extent. Just being open to it, is the first step to take.

During that weekend we also did some experimental dream work. Considering that I normally had some of the most bizarre dreams you could imagine, I was delighted to hear this. Maybe I would begin to understand what my dreams meant. One exciting thing we did was dream *for* someone in our group. I didn't know this could be possible. We were given special instructions on what to do that evening before we fell asleep.

I remember writing her name down on a piece of paper and putting it under my pillow. When I awoke I was to write everything down about the dream, only start from the end of the dream and work backwards to record as much as I could remember. Although I couldn't recall the exact dream, I do remember being amazed at the fact that fifteen people had all had dreams that related to the person's life for whom we were dreaming. I now had acquired some real tools to possibly help me along my path. This weekend was a success—the guest speakers were phenomenal and gave excellent presentations. It was a positive and unique experience all around, one that I will always be grateful for.

Returning from the conference, I decided to work on focusing on the positive around me. Hopefully this would lead to seeing favorable visions as opposed to the negative and sad flashes that seemed to continually emerge. This wasn't going to be an easy task since I didn't know how to stop what was coming through. Meditation seemed to be a good option. Something, anything, was needed to bring about a more calming state of mind and meditation claimed this was possible. Reading a number of books made me smile and even cringe over some of the possible meditation practices. I knew I couldn't sit like a pretzel, so that discipline was out. I couldn't see lighting a candle or incense each and every time either, was that really necessary? Controlled breathing seemed to be an important step, and I could handle that. It took time and practice to find a way that felt comfortable to me, all the while making my own adjustments. I began to meditate daily and ask my Spirit guides on the other side to help me. If they were going to show me something then go easy on me. Surely they would curtail the scary scenes of death flashing in my mind's eye? *Of course they would, wouldn't they?* Unfortunately, someone on the other side had a hearing problem or they weren't paying attention to my new state-of-mind theory.

Waking up to a chilly February morning made me feel warm and grateful to be at home. Each morning I would try to find time to meditate even if only for ten minutes. Along the way I found myself writing my thoughts on paper as they popped up during meditation. This became an exercise I enjoyed, and what emerged was often a surprise. Sometimes a grocery list, sometimes a tidbit to share with a loved one, I wrote down whatever came to me. There was nothing too small or too big to put on paper and the writing became automatic at times. Many times I would be thinking about one thing but realize I was writing about something else. One morning my thoughts turned toward my father-in-law as he lay in the hospital while time ticked by slowly. He had been there eighteen days so far and his heart and lungs were in conflict with his body. As I sat in meditation something made me ask a question instead of my usual practice of seeing what came to me. I asked out loud, "How is Paul today?" And my hand, as if it became separate from my body, wrote back: *He's going to die today.* Stiffening as I stared at the message on the paper before me, I threw the pen away as if it were on fire. Oh my God, that can't be right. I couldn't believe it. I just sat there. With that the phone rang. It was Carl telling me to get up to the hospital right away that they thought this might be it. I knew in my heart it was. I threw the pad of paper aside and got to the hospital as fast as I could. The family took turns going in to see Paul. Early that evening a few of us were sitting in his room watching, praying and waiting. Suddenly he sat up, leaned to the left, one leg moving to the side of the bed, and then his body fell backwards, landing safely on the comforting sheets. All of us jumped since he had hardly moved the entire day. I just sat there in awe of the moment. I intuitively knew he had just walked over to the other side leaving behind only the shell of his body. His soul had moved on. For me, it was a strangely beautiful moment that I was given the honor to witness. It should have been so painful to know he left us, because he was such a big wonderful man who gave the best bear hugs you can imagine. Instead it was the first time I felt honored with my gift. Being blessed to be one of the three sitting there to see him sit up in bed and just "walk away" felt like an honor. Although it took hours for his body to completely let go, I knew he already left us for the bright lights I saw shimmering around him to be with his loving relatives who were waiting for him.

***

I experienced the passing of my father-in-law an arm's length away, unlike previous death visions that seemed to flash in my mind out of nowhere. It's possible I was able to accept his death because the doctors prepared us somewhat in advance. We were fortunate to have a little time to spend with him and say good-bye in our own silent way. Other visions of death continued to haunt me and were difficult to accept as they became more common. It was extremely burdensome to know beforehand when someone was going to die. I have no doubt many people out there say it isn't possible, but then they probably don't have visions either. I wasn't crazy, even though sometimes it felt that way. I had loved ones to support what

I was envisioning, but no one to explain *why* I was experiencing this. So I went through my twenties struggling with the visions I was seeing and only sharing them with a few loved ones who understood me. Premonitions of death aren't something you go around talking about. When getting together with friends the conversation revolved around family, jobs, wines, food and any number of everyday events. Death wasn't really the topic of choice for your average conversation. So when dealing with a vision that would arise while with friends, I didn't share what I saw. Instead, I did the best I could to contain any emotions that arose. Over time a noticeable pattern began to emerge—from knowing months in advance, then to weeks and then to days, I would know when someone was going to die. It would hit me like a bomb, leaving my emotions fragmented when I would first see and feel it, never knowing whose turn it would be. A loved one's or friend's face would suddenly flash before me while I was doing the most mundane task, and then a second vision usually appeared prior to their demise. The lines would be blurry, so I never knew the exact place, or circumstance, but I saw enough to know death was coming. A car accident, an emergency surgical procedure gone bad, an unlikely drowning—all situations you would think could be prevented. How many times has someone told you to be careful when driving, check the surgeon's record before a procedure, or wear a life jacket? And yet, how many times do these words hang on deaf ears? It was difficult to handle and a nervous breakdown was imminent. Suffering through the waiting period until that day arrived left me feeling constantly off balance and out of sorts. Inappropriate as it may sound, a weight was lifted from me once the death came to pass. Eventually I developed a few psychic survival skills when dealing with the visions. Instead of waiting and worrying, I began to take control. Breaking it down according to days seemed to offer some direction. At the time of the vision I gave it three days. If death didn't occur within those three days, it usually wasn't going to happen, so then I could breathe again. I often cried from sheer joy on that third day! I chose to no longer watch the news since I could personally envision more than was being shown on TV. A news flash about an accident victim or murdered body wasn't something I felt I could handle at this time. Internally, fear and anger directed at myself was at a boiling point. Frustration that I couldn't stop or control what I experienced led to occasional depression because I couldn't "get past it." It was wearing me down and I just wanted it to stop.

My life may have seemed quite normal to those around me, but to me it was a mine field. Normal everyday life one minute, raising my son and enjoying life, then having my world explode. I had no idea where this path was leading me, but I knew that something had to change. I had to learn how to stop, or control, or at least try to understand the purpose of all this. Waking up every morning, already filled with anxiety, I wondered if a vision would manifest and what I would see. I needed help, but was afraid to ask for it. Being put on medicine to help me relax wasn't an option I was looking for, nor did I think going to the church I belonged to would help me either. I craved answers, not some man telling me God has big plans for me or a psychiatrist telling me I needed antipsychotics. Surely they would all agree I was delusional, but I knew I wasn't. Realistically, I couldn't walk up to someone and say "Listen, you're going to die soon, I'm not exactly sure how, but you might want to be careful and get your papers in order because it usually happens within a three day period from now." Imagine the reaction you'd receive. A twenty-something psychic with terrifying partial visions has no right to distress someone. I was in a situation where I wanted to help, yet didn't know how. I'd read about psychics and mediums who saved people from imminent death, and my comparative inactivity would make me feel even worse. Others were saving people and all I could do was pray and hope I was wrong. Why was life so cruel to me? Maybe my spiritual circuit was wired incorrectly. Meditation became crucial, and when praying I asked for direction and then told the Big Guy to get on the hot line and send help fast. Low and behold I think they heard me! Okay, so maybe there wasn't a hearing problem going on up there after all!

An acquaintance told me about a woman named Gerry who did Past Life Regression Hypnotherapy, which takes you back to a previous life where you confront issues that may continue to arise in this life. I imagined it as cleaning out the cobwebs in the attic of my mind and soul. Sounds fascinating, so why not give it a shot? Maybe she can help me find some answers. It wasn't the most conventional route, but my life hadn't exactly been conventional. So in the summer of 1994 I made my move and called her. I set up an appointment and when I arrived, explained my situation. She was very understanding and willing to help however she could. She saw the pain I was in and hoped as well that we could find some answers. Most importantly, she didn't judge me. We had a handful of interesting sessions. Past life regression wasn't what I thought it would be. There were no famous people that appeared or lives that I could boast about, however there was one life that stood out to me. I was a holy man with extremely long dark black hair, who had his legs cut off at the knees for speaking the truth when told not to. He seemed to be some sort of holy or spiritual advisor to a prominent man in the village nearby. This holy man dwelled in what looked to be a jungle setting in a small hut with few amenities. Whether this actually took place or was a subconscious creation of mine I can't be sure. On some level it rings true. It seems at least possible that seeing things I'm afraid to speak of may have origins in a past life. It sounds a bit farfetched unless you're living my life. Throughout the sessions I continued to have disturbing visions of people dying. The visions did slow down for a while but then picked up once again. I felt regression work helped, but it wasn't helping in the area in which I needed it most. I asked Gerry if there was any other technique I could try that might possibly help me and she suggested Holotropic Breathwork™, which was created by Stanislav and Christina Grof. This technique was created to induce non-ordinary states of consciousness and to gain access to the unconscious and super conscious psyche. It sounded amazing and unique and something that possibly would trigger a shift for me. I was willing to give it a try, and among other things it not only gave me a key to a new world, but helped me see that death isn't the end of the story.

Chapter Three
The Prodigious Breathwork

Do not go where the path may lead, go instead
where there is no path and leave a trail.
Ralph Waldo Emerson

Fall of 1994 my sister Debbie and I decided to try Holotropic Breathwork. We entered the red brick building where it would take place. Walking up the steps one by one carrying my blanket felt like I was climbing a mountain, it was a new adventure and I wondered what lay in store for me. Adrenaline was building as the hallway appeared before me and my walking became quicker in anticipation. I turned into the room where the Holotropic Breathwork would take place and saw pale blue walls and mauve carpet. Cedar incense was burning off to the side and the lighting was low, bathing the room with a warm glow. Numerous people had already arrived and taken their spot on the floor where room was available. Debbie and I walked over to an empty area and set our blankets down following their lead. We had been told earlier the day would be divided into two sessions. First a morning session, where one of us would experience the Holotropic Breathwork while the other sat next to the participant, assisting them if they needed anything. I was a little confused by this, and I wondered what they could possibly need. If they got cold, maybe cover them with the blanket? If they started coughing, maybe a glass of water? I didn't know what else I could do but I would find out soon enough. When finished with the first part, the participant would move to another room and draw their mandala. Drawing on a large square piece of paper, with a circle in the center, they would create a picture of their experience using colored pencils or pastels to express their Holotropic Breathwork in visual form. After that, participants could choose to enjoy a light snack if needed and then the afternoon session would commence. We decided Debbie would take the first session. She lay down and got situated on her blanket, as I sat next to her on mine. The lights were dimmed to where you could just barely see shapes and forms of those around you and the music was turned on low. The cedar incense drifted through the length of the room tantalizing the senses. The facilitator began the breathing exercises and then the volume to the music was elevated to a pitch that could make you lose yourself within it. It was evoking, pulling and pushing my thoughts around as I could only imagine what Debbie was feeling. The emotions in the room were heating the place up even though the air conditioning was blasting out of the vent nearby. Looking around, I saw movement, some curling up in their blankets or rolling back and forth and twisting around. Others made noises and I wondered, *"What was their story... everyone has one."* Time drifted for me and sitting there for my sister was easy, she really didn't require anything from me. I did cover her up once, so at least I didn't feel totally useless. Before I knew it the session was over. What seemed like 15 minutes was actually over an hour and a half. I had been so busy taking in everything around me time had ticked by swiftly. Although I watched my sister on and off, it looked like she was peacefully napping, but then again I wasn't going through her experience, so who was I to say what was really going on? When the Holotropic Breathwork was over Debbie and the other participants got up slowly and went into the other room to sit quietly and draw their mandala while the rest of us got ready for our session. I brought Debbie some juice she asked for and silently walked out of the room, glancing around amazed at what everyone was drawing. There seemed to be many experiences that took place that I didn't see or must have missed! In the circle of one participant's mandala were flames of a fire out of control, another had an expression of a rainbow in beautiful pastel colors splashing around which made me smile. And then I saw others who drew things that were evolving into an abstract creation of some form. Seeing this made me wonder what had happened for them and what would happen for me?

The afternoon session was about to begin. I said a silent prayer to whoever was listening to help me stop seeing terrible visions. Give me something concrete to help me in some way. The facilitator walked into the room. She lit incense, patchouli this time and then dimmed the lights. I laid down and got comfortable as Debbie now sat beside me quietly. The breathing exercises began. Closing my eyes, focusing on my breath, I could hear music slowly surround me and fill the walls to capacity. Relaxed... so relaxed... and far away from the world around me... drifting within a bubble... isolated from the outside world. I heard rustling around me, someone crying—it didn't seem to affect me in the least. I slowly felt an energy invade my space, it was one of comfort, and I felt an odd shifting take place. It felt so incredible to just exist, to feel life without the cloud of heavy emotion and I was savoring the moment. Time stood still. I was floating in a vast sea of tranquility. No pain, no sorrow, and no visions of death, only peace and freedom. I just wanted to stay in this cocoon of comfortable warm light forever and forget the outside world. This was Nirvana. Gradually I felt a change around me as if I was slowly emerging from the cocoon I was occupying. Acknowledging my spirit felt free like a butterfly's, although my body lay motionless oblivious to my spirit's flight. My Holotropic Breathwork was coming to an end. Slowly, drifting back and returning to normality, my eyes opened and I felt that I emerged with a radiance of peaceful energy shooting out of every pore, overlain with a sense of intrigue. Something very powerful was going on here, something never previously experienced in my life. A freedom to let go—like a wind vane shifting directions, my sense of self started to change directions. There was such contentment and I immediately wanted to experience it again, if only to immerse myself within the atmosphere of that peaceful space. Debbie helped me up, and then followed me into the other room and made sure I was okay, then left quietly to get me some tea. A large piece of paper lay before me, stark white, glaring up at me, waiting to see what colors I would place upon it. What emerged from my fingers and onto my mandala were shades of yellows, golds and oranges, bright beautiful colors, my interpretation of rays of light and energy. Pleased with my finished product, I got up, grabbed the mandala I created and walked back into the other room. Debbie was folding the blankets and some people were beginning to leave while others stayed around and sat in a circle to discuss their Holotropic Breathwork. We decided to sit and listen but didn't share much from our experiences—we both felt our personal experiences were something we needed to digest before we shared them with others. No decision was needed, without a second thought we signed up for a session the following month. I couldn't wait to see what would happen next, hoping I might encounter a similar experience, or maybe experience something even more amazing.

October...1994

A day engraved in my memory forever.

Debbie and I arrived for our second Holotropic Breathwork. She parked the car and we jumped out in anticipation, grabbing our bags and heading toward the red brick building. I opened the door and we hustled up the stairs and made our way into the same room with the light blue walls and pale mauve carpet, an average room by anyone's standards. There wasn't anything that stood out about it, except the fact I could never forget it.

We chose a place in the corner of the room and laid out our blankets and the pillows we decided to bring as well. We previously decided Debbie would once again go first. People were spreading out around us and in front of us. The corner was an ideal spot, because whoever was not participating in the Holotropic Breathwork had a wall to lean against. As I observed the people around us, I realized that there wasn't anything unusual about them. They looked like anyone you would see walking down the street, pumping gas or buying a sandwich at the local deli. But as I said before, everyone has a history and a reason for seeking.

The facilitator came in and she turned the lights down low, lit incense, cedar again and began the music. She started with the breathing exercises and the mood in the room shifted. It wasn't long before I felt I was living in an electrical storm of human energy. Emotions were flashing across the room like lightning as music thundered through the soul. As Debbie laid on her blanket and began her experience, I glanced around the room and had a feeling of being somehow connected to everyone in the world. I was overwhelmed. Here I sat in this small room, located in a non-descript red-brick building you might find anywhere in the Midwest, connected by another state of consciousness to the whole universe. I was this tiny speck on the map and yet the connection I was feeling went far beyond our world. I found the morning's session engrossing and inspiring, even though I had yet to go through the Breathwork. As I drifted in and out of my thoughts the morning session was coming to an end. Soon everyone was moving off to the other room. I helped Debbie up off the blanket since she looked a little dazed and we walked into the other room so she could draw her mandala as others were doing with chalk, pencils, markers or paints.

While Debbie drew her thoughts onto the poster board, I left and walked back into the blue and mauve room. Being the tidy person I am, I folded her blanket and repositioned the pillow. My blanket was already in order and so I walked over to chat with a couple of the sitters while we waited for time to pass. I watched the clock impatiently as it slowly ticked by to the voices of those around me. I could still feel a residue of electric energy in the room, as if you could reach out and literally grab it, and wondered if the others felt the same way. If so no one mentioned it. I thought about what I saw and hoped that most, if not all, found the answers they were searching for. My anticipation made time drag by at a crawling pace. Eventually, people slowly filtered back into the room. When Debbie walked in, I got up from where I was sitting with the others and went back to my blanket.

The short break was over. The time I was waiting for had finally arrived. Lying down, I expressed my thoughts to Debbie by asking her to not stare at me during my Holotropic Breathwork. I mean, who knows what kinds of faces I might make? Some of the others scattered around the room had made quite a variety of contorted faces and movements during the morning session. Being my sister, she just silently gave me the look that says a thousand words. I smiled back, closed my eyes and relaxed. Let's get this show on the road, I thought. I sent up a silent prayer, like I did at home right before I left, to please give me something tangible today, to help me survive my visions. I knew I had something big going on. Let me understand and not fear them, or make the visions go away and give me some peace.

The music began, and was instantly evocative, pulling me into a place where I felt like a piece of artwork. I noticed through my closed eyelids that the lights had dimmed, then the facilitator started the breathing exercises. The music embraced me, a synesthesic experience, and I relaxed—floating, weightless, just like my previous Holotropic Breathwork session, in a soft haze, and then a cocoon of light surrounding me. Suddenly, the background chatter faded to a murmur that ended in silence. I let go of any preconceived notion of what I hoped to experience. It was so peaceful to not think of anything, to simply live in the stillness, the oneness of the moment. I wanted to stay that way forever.

Suddenly, from across the room I heard a scream and it pierced my place of warmth. I was stunned by the agonizing sorrow the voice brought.

31

I began to converse within, and asked myself, "Why am I here? Am I doing the right thing?" I slowly drifted off again to that bright warm spot and just basked in the peacefulness of it, when I began to hear an unidentifiable voice from far away and to my left. Quickly, it accelerated approaching closer and suddenly a message came through as a whisper, but loud and clear: Janet, get up and go to the bathroom!

Moving, as if on automatic pilot, I jumped up and told Debbie I had to go to the bathroom. As soon as the words left my mouth, I thought, "Why in the heck am I going to the bathroom? Who told me to do that?" I knew what she was thinking. I wasn't a little kid anymore and should have known better. I don't know why I jumped up, I just acted on command. Debbie guided me around the people sprawled across the floor and out the door to the bathroom across the hall. Afterward, I walked to the sink to wash my hands and looked in the mirror, all the while wondering *who* had told me to head toward the bathroom. I had never heard that voice before. It came though as an order but also as a request. Confused over this turn in my Holotropic Breathwork, I slowly moved back into the room feeling so off balance that I needed help back onto my blanket. I vaguely wondered again who had spoken to me. To her credit, Debbie didn't say a word about this incident, and she had no clue that anyone had whispered to me.

As I lay down I suddenly felt this energy similar to before, only it became stronger and stronger, all around me and then within me, building as it went along. I felt pressure in my chest, which moved to my throat and out of my mouth with a force of its own. Exceeding the impossible, the unimaginable transpired—I began spontaneously speaking a language I had never heard before. SA-LA-MAY-PAY, SA-LA-MAY-PAY. Words flew off my tongue, the power behind them staggering. I began speaking so fast that I had little control over my tongue, but I was never afraid. SA-LA-MAY-PAY, I felt elated, overjoyed as if something wonderful was taking place within. My voice was thunderous, vibrating as I shouted and screamed, laughing and crying as I rejoiced! I began slowing down, taking a breath, then once again building, gaining speed and incredible strength—like the force of an arrow shot from a bow, the unknown words flew from my lips, propelling me into a sitting position so that the language could run its course through my upper body. As if I had been hibernating in my life until this very moment in time, it emerged like a hungry bear. The pressure inside was something I had never experienced before. It was contradictory: euphoric and turbulent all entwined. I somehow knew that the words formed a message whose purpose I felt but couldn't explain. My tongue was moving so fast, but I had no idea what was being said. My body would shift from side to side for reasons I couldn't imagine. My hands were holding my chest as the intense energy emerged, then fluttered about as if to express something important.

Abruptly my tongue would halt, and then begin a chant that was poetic. I could hear myself as if I was within and outside myself at the same time. I couldn't help feel that a door had opened within me. Flashes of light, trees and unfamiliar people danced across a movie screen in my mind. On and on, I voiced a message that needed to be set free, to be released from its origins. I was exhilarated and without fear, experiencing infinite bliss. I let this unknown language carry me through this unknown world of confusing beauty. I wanted to feel this way forever and share whatever was being said with everyone. Gradually, gently, I felt a change deep within me and knew the experience was drawing to a close. The Holotropic Breathwork was coming to an end. When I slowly found my way back, I opened my eyes and looked up only to see Debbie staring down at me in shock. I stared into her eyes and saw disbelief and confusion mirrored back at me.

I started to say something but realized my throat was raw and I had just about lost my voice. So I sat up, looking around the room. Everyone was staring at me like I had ten heads. Not that it really mattered, nothing did at this point. I didn't care who had seen me, what just happened was extraordinary and beyond my ability to comprehend. If I couldn't comprehend it, how could they?

I was encouraged to get up and go draw my mandala immediately, but I was so shaky that Debbie had to hold my arm as we walked sluggishly into the other room. My body was drained of energy, as if I had been depleted down to the last cell in my body. I sat down in front of a piece of paper with a circle drawn on it. I was drawn to a piece of deep dark green chalk. Picking it up, I put my hand to paper. Then I suddenly had so much energy running through me that my hands began to shake almost uncontrollably! I tried to relax, but my hand began to move on its own accord. It began moving up and down, but not left to right, making lines, dashes and slashes on the paper. My hand moved with an energy of its own, line after line, from top to bottom. The sound of the pastel chalk hitting the paper beat out a hypnotic harmony. When I finished, my mandala was made up of nothing other than lines and angles, a sea of jungle green on a white canvas. I hadn't a clue what it meant, if anything at all. I had been a bystander as I watched my hand work, just as I had been when my own voice spoke. Dazed, I sat there numb, staring at the room around me and seeing nothing.

What just happened? What the hell just happened? Where did this come from?

Didn't I have enough going on without this overwhelming, amazing and confusing experience? Didn't I have enough on my damn plate already?

But like it or not, another journey began…

PART II

The Language

Chapter Four

The Journey

The important thing is not to stop questioning.
Albert Einstein

"Debbie, let's get out of here," I quickly suggested, as we walked back into the blue and mauve room.

"Yeah, good idea," she replied.

Holding my mandala, I grabbed my blanket and pillow while Debbie gathered her things and we ducked out before anyone could comment or question what had happened to me. I wasn't in the mood to talk. Hell, I wasn't sure what had just happened. I couldn't wrap my thoughts around much at this point, much less intelligently discuss it. Walking down the stairs Debbie asked, "Are you okay?"

"I'm still shaky, but I think so. Good thing you're driving."

"Well if I wasn't, I would be now," she chuckled.

"Good point."

We got into Debbie's car and I threw my blanket and pillow in the back, but held on to my mandala as if it were a life source. "What the hell just happened in there Debbie?"

"Well," she replied cautiously, "It sounds like you were speaking some type of foreign language."

"Yeah I agree, but what? Why? How? God, I'm so confused. It was so cool and amazing and surreal. It felt like someone came through me and manipulated my vocal cords to get some kind of message across. It felt important. It felt liberating. Man that was wild. But why me?"

"I don't know why you, maybe everything in the past brought you here to this moment."

"Yeah maybe, but maybe it was a quirk of fate never to happen again. This is so bizarre, but so cool. Man, how am I going to explain this one to Carl," I laughed.

"You'll think of something, I'm sure. Besides, do you really think he'll be that surprised by anything you tell him after all you've been through?"

"Yeah, well this is different. How do you tell someone that you have someone else talking through you? I'm still shaking... I feel excited like I just ate a pound of chocolate and topped it with an espresso or two. If this is what it feels like to be high, man, I don't want to come down!" I said jokingly.

Debbie laughed, "Janet that was so wild, at first I thought you were whispering to me, so I leaned over, then you started talking louder and when you sat up you almost hit me. I just can't believe that happened. You'll have to call me if it happens again."

"Believe me, if it happens again, you'll know," I said.

"And hey, sorry I was looking at you when you came out of your Breathwork. I know you told me not to, but after what happened I think you'll agree that was impossible."

"No problem, I would have done the same."

"Then I guess it's okay to tell you a number of people walked over and were watching you."

"Quite a show, huh?" I muttered.

"Yes it was. Make sure after all that, that you ground yourself. Eat a big hamburger or something and drink plenty of water."

"Yes, mom," I said sarcastically.

"I'm just reminding you Janet, you've been through quite a lot in the last couple of hours."

"Yeah I know, I'll make sure I eat and drink something, thanks for the reminder."

After that, we sat quietly, watching the scenery pass by, both lost in our thoughts of what we had experienced that day.

As Debbie pulled into my driveway I was thinking how I couldn't believe how much my life seemed to change in just a matter of hours. You just never know what will happen from one minute to the next. I just didn't think life would throw me such a curve ball. Earlier today I was hoping to get some answers or insight about why I was seeing visions of people dying and now I'm home with something else to wonder about.

"Debbie, I'm so glad you were there with me today," I said as I reached for my blanket and pillow.

"Me too," she replied, "If you need anything, give me a call."

"Okay, I will, thanks."

I gave her a hug and bounced out of the car and hurried up the sidewalk to the front door. Letting myself in, I looked around. Everything seemed the same, yet a little different. Maybe it was just because I was still so hyper. Carl and our son, Matt, weren't home yet. They were at Carl's Mom's house for Sunday dinner, a tradition I missed this week because of the Holotropic Breathwork. So, I went in and took a shower, put on comfy clothes and tried to relax until they got home. It didn't work. By the time they walked through the door, I was still a bundle of nerves. TV and channel changing didn't seem to calm me, nor pacing through the house. I finally plopped into a chair. Sitting, legs crossed, I began swinging the one up and down, triggering a reminder of when my grandma would use one of her favorite comments—I was digging my grave. Wondering where that thought came from, a smirk inched across my face. Was Grandma coming from the grave to offer me comfort? I could use some. What happened earlier in the day was starting to sink in. Well, at least as much as I could comprehend anyway. Carl could see I was restless as I spent the evening playing with Matt. Surprisingly he didn't ask how my day went. It didn't matter since he was going to find out soon enough.

After putting Matt to bed, I walked back into the great room and told him, "We need to talk."

"I figured you would tell me about your day once Matt went to sleep," he said.

"Yeah well, it was quite a day," I said and went on to tell him exactly what happened.

When I finished, he waved me over to sit next to him and I curled up against him for comfort. The day had taken its toll and I found myself exhausted and decided to go to bed.

As I lay down, my last thought was how odd it was that Carl never asked me anything after I told him I spontaneously began speaking a foreign language.

A new day began; Carl was scheduled for the evening shift so we made plans to spend the day running errands. After a night to digest my story, he now had many questions. I thought to myself, *it was about damn time!* Hell, I would have been quizzing him until midnight. It wasn't until we dropped our son off at preschool that Carl began asking the questions that had been consuming his thoughts.

"You called this a language, but how do you know it is one?" he asked.

I thought about it and said, "I don't know for sure that it is a language, but it sounds like one and more importantly it felt like one, as if someone was talking through me and had an important message that they had to get out. I don't know—compare it to someone speaking a foreign language to you. You may not know what they are saying, but by the tone, and the way they move you can grasp some sort of intention from it." With this, I just know it's a language, carrying an important message.

"So, were you scared?"

"No, I wasn't at all. It was so incredible, I just felt all this power emerge up through my chest and through my vocal cords, then out of my mouth and the whole time my tongue felt so foreign. Like it was moving differently than normal, which I guess it was."

"Did it hurt when you felt it in your chest?"

"No, but it was strange, like someone was pushing or pulling something out of me. Maybe manipulating something within me, does that sound stupid?" I said.

"No, but I'm having a hard time understanding what you felt since I've never heard of this happening before, and can't really imagine it happening at all."

"Yeah, I guess. I'm not sure what to think either but it was so cool. I mean you can't imagine when it started happening, it just sort of took over my upper body and I was feeling it, but also at times I felt outside of it as if watching myself from the side, then moving back and forth as if my body could expand or shift. I know that sounds crazy, even to me, but that's how I felt." I replied.

"Why do you think it happened?" he asked next.

"It felt like there was an important message of some kind, that had to come through me in the way it did, I just have no clue what it was. What's so perplexing is that I'm not afraid at all. Maybe because it just felt so wonderful. I mean it's right up there with getting married and having a baby. It was just that awesome."

"So, do you think you can speak it again?"

I looked over at him in the car and said, "Ya know, I have no idea."

And with that my tongue began to jerk, as if someone pulled on it or put tiny weights on it. It got heavy.

"Carl, my tongue is feeling strange, maybe I can! I'll try to see if I can speak it for a couple of minutes."

I closed my eyes to concentrate but it wasn't needed because I spontaneously began speaking it rapidly right in the car while Carl was driving down the highway. The language flowed through my vocal cords like creamy butter, but tumbled off my tongue choppy like the rough sea on a windy day. And then it stopped just as quickly. I opened my eyes, looked over at Carl and was in awe of the moment.

"You spoke for exactly two minutes. I glanced at the clock when you started and you said you would try it for a couple minutes. How did you do that?" Carl exclaimed nervously.

"No clue," I said in amazement, "it just seems to have stayed with me. I had no idea I could even speak it again. Wow, this is bizarre."

"That's an understatement, but I guess I'm not surprised. You always have weird stuff happening around you." Carl said, "I'm just having a hard time believing what just happened."

I smiled and said, "Me too, I had no idea I could still speak it."

When we finished our errands he headed over to my Mom's house. We had a little time before we had to pick up Matt from school and I wanted to share with Mom what happened. Luckily we caught her at home—with being a successful real estate agent, you never knew. I asked her to sit down because I had something really important to tell her. She smiled, probably thinking I was going to tell her I was pregnant again. That wasn't the news she was about to receive. I began to explain how I attended a Holotropic Breathwork and went on to explain what that was, then told her something unusual happened.

"Mom, I began speaking some sort of language during the Holotropic Breathwork."

"What do you mean?"

"Well, I spontaneously began speaking a language that sounded foreign and I realized today I can still speak it. Would you like to hear it?" I said.

She looked at me cautiously and said, "All right."

I closed my eyes self-consciously and began speaking immediately. The language that emerged was fluid in its simplicity as it moved up through my chest, difficult to form as it crossed my tongue. I felt strong emotions build throughout my upper body once again, then rush past my lips speaking words I have never heard and words I didn't understand, yet knew they held a message. It felt so right, it just felt so right. When I finished I opened my eyes and looked at Mom. She had an animated look on her face and I could tell she wanted to say something, but didn't know what. This was not so surprising considering the circumstances, so I asked, "Well, what do you think?"

Stunned, she said, "Oh my God Janet, that's pretty amazing. Do you know what that means?"

"No idea Mom, I just started speaking it. It's so wild."

"Well, I don't fully understand it, but I'll admit it's pretty exciting. A little odd to hear my daughter speaking a foreign language she never studied. I hope you find out what it means."

"Me too Mom," I replied.

"Well, if I can do anything to help, let me know."

"I will, thanks Mom," I said.

The response I received from Mom was positive as I knew it would be. My Mom is the best. Even when she doesn't understand it, she is still behind me and offering support. Even if she did think I might be heading toward some serious counseling she didn't suggest it. With hindsight, that might have been a good idea.

The days afterward rolled by in a comfortable pattern. I started speaking *the language* as I called it, spontaneously many times throughout the week, never knowing but always wondering what was being said. It became a form of comfort. Maybe because it felt so incredible when it came through, like I had won the lottery and I was doing a happy dance inside. Every time it came through, it brought happiness and joy.

On a chilly afternoon, standing at the stove, preparing potato soup, I began singing like I often do when I cook. I'm not sure what made me take notice, but I suddenly became aware that I was singing in *the language* which up until that point I didn't know was possible. I couldn't believe it, it just emerged and flowed like a melody I had known for years, but I had never heard it before. Carl and Matt walked in from the snowy outdoors and glanced towards me to hear me singing in this language while stirring my homemade soup.

Carl jokingly asked, "Are you singing about soup?"

"I have no clue, I guess I could be." I laughed in wonder.

Maybe whoever was coming through was performing a ceremony of some sort, which was parallel to my stirring soup over a hot fire. Needless to say it was a delightful afternoon with yet another aspect of the language unveiled.

As a family we were all getting used to this near daily scene. At age four my son assumed this was just something normal. And so he became used to hearing it as if it was nothing special. I also noticed at this time that I wasn't seeing any visions of people dying. It gave me a new burst of energy to think that this language somehow had changed my focus. I felt more positive as well. I went from seeing tragic scenes before they happened to suddenly nothing at all! This astounding language was a turning point. Giving credit where credit was due, there was a definite shift within me when the language manifested. It's possible I spent so much time focusing on the language that I never allowed the disturbing visions to break through. This was a good thing, a very good thing. I gave thanks to the unseen for allowing this language to materialize.

Days later, after telling most of my family about the language and receiving positive feedback, I thought it was time to tell my in-laws. I began with my Mother-in-law, a frightening thought to many I'm sure, but it was just the opposite. Hermina is a classy lady who has always been open and interested in my intuitive experiences that I had shared with her over the years. So, Carl, Matt and I drove over early one Sunday afternoon before our traditional Sunday dinner. Hermina and I sat around the kitchen table chatting while Matt went off to play in the other room with Carl, who kept an eye on the football scores. The kitchen has always been the gathering place and its warmth and comfort were a perfect backdrop. Excited, I had just begun to share my story about the language coming though when a distant relative dropped by for a visit. Clare is one of my favorites, so I started the story over to share my new-found discovery with her as well. When I was finished, my Mother-in-law was astonished and although she could think of no immediate explanation, she was enthusiastic and delighted for me. Clare, on the other hand, said nothing. I didn't think anything of it since I had also been thunderstruck when it first happened. I continued with, "Would you like to hear me speak it?" I knew they would of course.

"Sure," Hermina responded, while Clare stated a vehement "No!"

I was surprised as I glanced over at Clare asking her, "Why not?"

Staring at me with eyes widened, she replied, "Do you even know what you're saying? It could be the work of the Devil!"

That wasn't all she had to say as I stared back at her with shock written across my face. "Janet, it may harm my unborn baby!"

43

I was rendered speechless. After a five-second pause, my brain once again began to function. *Is she serious?* I silently thought. Words began to form as I said, "You're right, I don't know for sure what it means, but I don't think this language would harm anyone Clare. It feels phenomenal when I speak it. If anything, it's a blessing. It feels positive and right, like a sacred spiritual energy coming through with an important message."

She didn't agree and left the room stating, "Just in case."

I tried not to show how hurt and baffled I was, although truth be told, I was blown away by her comments. I turned to Hermina and asked, "Do you still want to hear me speak the language?"

"Of course I do, and Janet just ignore Clare, maybe she is just going through some hormonal changes with being pregnant."

"Yeah, okay," I whispered and tried to act like everything was fine.

Starting to speak this new language, I realized I had my eyes open as I watched Hermina's response. She was totally open minded and was smiling when I finished.

"That's beautiful!" she exclaimed.

"Thanks Hermina." I leaned over to give her a hug.

"I appreciate you listening to it."

"It's very interesting Janet. I wonder what you're saying," she replied.

"I wonder too!"

It was time for Hermina to finish preparing dinner and for me to set the table. Soon everyone arrived and joined in helping with dinner preparations. After the incident with Clare, I decided not to mention the language to anyone at dinner and contemplate the situation instead. As the evening ended and we were heading back home I sat in the car silently trying to deal with these new-found emotions that had surfaced after Clare's comments. Since the moment this language first emerged I had been enthralled and consumed by it. It never crossed my mind that anyone would think differently, especially in a negative sense. Clare's comments literally stopped me in my tracks and made me wonder if others would feel the same way. She taught me an important lesson tonight, one I didn't want, but one I obviously needed to hear. The rejection I felt from hearing her remarks was extremely upsetting, but I tried not to show it. She hadn't meant to hurt me, but her knee jerk response made me wonder if her comments had derived from fear. I've lived with so many of my own fears, I understand what it could do and how it made me feel. So, who am I to judge someone else? I realized I had to let go of the fact I equated her rejection with not having faith in myself. Most likely I had triggered her own personal fears. It's understandable that someone who has always had strongly structured beliefs might not understand something so out of the ordinary. I decided the best thing to do is accept her beliefs for what they are, let go of my feeling of rejection and move on. Besides, there couldn't be too many others who have Clare's belief, could there?

A week later, Carl and I had some friends over for the evening. We've been friends with this couple for many years and they are the type you could walk around with holes in your shirt and bed head and they wouldn't mind. We've sat up many nights until dawn talking about anything from sports to travel to the latest product on the market for cleaning the shower. I decided to pull Sherry aside and tell her about the language.

"Sherry, you're not going to believe what happened to me," I said with excitement in my voice. I went on to explain what happened and gave her every last detail from the Holotropic Breathwork workshop.

"Oh Janet," she sighed, "Girl, you're such a lost soul and I'm going to pray for you."

Wow, her comment literally blew me away.

"Sherry," I said laughingly, "I'm not lost."

"Yes, you are. Why don't I make you an appointment with my pastor so you can speak with him. I'm sure he can help you with whatever you're going through."

"Um, well I really think I'm fine, but thanks for the offer," I said quietly, feeling hurt by her comment. It was difficult for the rest of the evening to put on a normal face, since her close-mindedness made me feel rejected. She wanted to "fix me" but I wasn't "broken." I was surprised that someone with self-professed religious values was so intolerant. If these two women could feel the amazement I felt every time the language emerged, they would be solidly on my side. Instead, one thought I was a devil woman and the other thought my soul was lost. Both they and I had been raised with traditional religious beliefs, but I had explored beyond them. They weren't being open to something extraordinary that was happening right in front of their eyes to someone they have known for years. I recognized that I was at a spiritual crossroad. Either I needed new family and friends, or I needed answers and fast!

I began to seek answers by calling the language department at Washington University in my home town of St. Louis. I explained to the woman on the phone who I was, my unusual circumstances and that I wanted to identify the language I was spontaneously speaking. She was open-minded and told me to send her a cassette tape of the language and she would see what she could do. Great! This was going to be easy, I thought, I would have my answers in no time at all!

About a week later she called to tell me the language wasn't known by any of the professors in her department, and that it definitely wasn't French, Spanish, Latin, German, Tibetan, Greek, Chinese, Japanese or Mongolian. She then advised me on where to send the tape next. It was a start! I thanked her for her kindness and moved on.

I next contacted the government agency she referred me to, one that later stated I couldn't cite their name for privacy reasons. After sending a tape and waiting weeks to hear back, I finally received a call. They explained they didn't recognize the language either, but I could rule out Aramaic, Arabic, Hebrew, Persian, Turkish and Gaelic. Well, this was progress, so I took out a world map and started crossing off areas from where those languages originated. However, if you cross out half of a world map, you still have one heck of an area to cover. I clearly had my work cut out for me. I was excited each time I sent my language tape somewhere new, then waiting in anticipation, only to be let down when I would receive a call or email. Patience isn't exactly my strong suit, but I had no choice but to continue. I believed with time and diligence that I would find someone who recognized this obviously exotic language. I tried to stay optimistic.

I continued to raise my son and have a normal family life while I diligently contacted universities throughout the United States. I even approached language clubs, linguistic groups and churches. Although no one knew what language I was speaking, I did receive a vast amount of personal and professional opinions. One man noted for his degrees in psychiatry, and the study of reincarnation thought my phenomenon might be glossolalia. Not knowing what that was I asked him to explain. He told me that glossolalia, also known as "speaking in tongue," consisted of either meaningless utterances of part of a holy language, depending on who was listening, and that it sometimes results from schizophrenia. Oh great, that's alarming to hear. I thanked him and hung up quickly. *Was this possible? Could I be schizophrenic and not know it?* That made me stop and think and I did extensive research to learn what the characterizations were. I came to understand how this gentleman might have associated my situation with glossolalia or even being schizophrenic, but I knew he was wrong and moved on toward an answer to my question.

Place after place, month after month, year after year, the results always came back the same, no one could identify the language I was speaking. Respectfully, many wished me luck on my journey. Even after four years of sending out my tape, I wasn't about to give up. That wasn't an option. I was willing to spend the rest of my life in this quest, because I was convinced that the language had come to me for an important purpose. At this point only my family, a few friends and scholars to whom I'd sent the tape knew about the language. However, I knew in my heart that someday I would find the answer.

I was living two lives—a normal one on the outside, and a private life with a secret language. Envisioning people die several days beforehand became mercifully rare. By being so focused on my quest, I think that I pushed my deathly visions to the background. My desire to share and learn this language vibrated from the core of my being. At times the dark outlook of others cast a shadow over my own sense of wonder and joy that this language brought forth. I chose not to allow their negativity to penetrate my soul and kept pushing forward.

More tapes, more emails—it became a full-time job that I added to my daily life. The turning point came when I emailed the Polynesian Cultural Center in Honolulu to ask if they would listen to my tape. A woman named Kim, replied back,

"Janet, we would be happy to pass your tape around. We have natives who are fluent in over twenty languages throughout the islands." She then listed where to send my tape.

I replied, "Thanks Kim, I appreciate your assistance. Looking forward to hearing from you soon."

Weeks passed, after scanning my emails for the hundredth time, Kim's arrived.

"Aloha Janet, I'm sorry to report your language is not any of our island languages. However, one of my co-workers just returned from South America. When she heard the tape she commented that it sounded similar to what she heard while on vacation. Best of luck," Kim.

I broke down and cried, reading the email over and over. I now had something tangible to hold on to. The language was real, I knew it was! I've searched for years, never giving up or giving in to others' negative opinions, and now I'm going to be rewarded with an answer. I was shaking. This was the first time in over four years anyone mentioned "my" language sounded similar to a language they'd actually heard. I could finally see a light at the end of the tunnel, and that tunnel was leading to South America!

With a new-found sense of direction, I searched online, and came across the website for the Institute of Noetic Science (IONS). I loved their magazine and they even offered a number of trips coincidently or not to

South America. I didn't know which IONS person to contact first. I had reached a pivotal moment, as if I knew that the person I contacted first would be instrumental in my journey. I sat repeating over and over the two names of the guides who led trips to South America. "Pick me, pick me," one name seemed to silently shout with a deafeningly roar. My decision was made. My fingers moved shakily as I clicked the white box at the top of the email next to the words, "Send to." The contrast of the name, "John Perkins" written in black, point 12, Times New Roman reverberated through my soul. It felt as if the world was going to start spinning in the opposite direction, or another equally dramatic action take place. I pressed, "Send."

Chapter Five

Crossing Paths

It takes two to speak the truth: one to speak, and another to hear.
Henry David Thoreau

I emailed John Perkins with my unusual story. I asked him as I had so many others to please listen to my tape and see if it sounded at all familiar to him. In a matter of hours I received a reply. "Send the tape" and he enclosed his address. As I mailed the tape off, I found it ironic that my tape had traveled to more places than I have. I worried that this was another dead end, but I tried to be optimistic, and in truth I felt a confidence in John as I hadn't in any previous person. Hopefully that feeling would hold true. Although the patience I've learned over the years helped me in the past, my current journey has provided a lot of wear and tear. I wasn't sure I could handle another rejection letter. The pile was collecting to what seemed like an insurmountable mountain. I had to keep going, because I felt there was a purpose to my journey. I feel it. Besides, I wasn't raised to give up if things don't go one's way.

A week later, early on a Friday morning, my phone rang. I had just finished getting ready for work and sat down with my usual cup of decaffeinated coffee. I jumped up to grab the phone on the second ring.

"Hello," I said.

"May I speak with Janet, please?" the voice on the other line asked.

"Speaking," I replied.

"Hello Janet, this is John Perkins."

"Oh! Hi Mr. Perkins, I guess you received my tape."

"Yes I did and please, call me John. I listened to your tape and believe I know what you're speaking. Before I say what that language is I would like to send it to a friend of mine if that would be alright." John asked.

"Of course, feel free to send it to whomever you wish." I exclaimed excitedly.

"Okay, then I'm going to send it to my friend Ipupiara. He's from South America. I believe you're speaking an indigenous Amazonian tribal language. He'll be able to verify it and possibly let you know what you're saying."

I could hardly hold the phone, shaking with uncontrollable emotion. My entire body seemed to have electrical currents running through it as he spoke.

"Yes, that would be great, thank you."

"I'll get it out to him soon and we'll see what he has to say," he said smoothly.

"Thank you, thank you I would appreciate that," I managed to say amid the pulsing beat of my heart pounding and drumming through my ears.

I realized I was at a loss for words, my mind was blank, no thoughts would emerge. Staring at the kitchen wall I was a million miles away. My breathing became labored and I had a sudden fear I might hyperventilate and pass out missing the rest of the conversation. Snap out of it, focus. As much as I wanted this, to hear it, to have an answer, it was still overwhelming. I've searched four and a half years, just waiting for this one phone call and in a snap of a finger I had an answer.

I not only found one person I was searching for, I might have found a second one who could translate what I'm saying. Unbelievable. I was shaking so uncontrollably as I held the phone to my ear, I was literally hitting myself with it. As if from a distance, I realized John had continued talking, explaining that he travels to a number of areas in South America. He's been traveling there since the 1960s and even lived in South America for a time. He knew a number of different tribes and a little of their languages. He spoke of how he was interested in the indigenous tribes and learning the ways of the shaman. Not only was I fortunate in finding out what area my language came from, but I'd met a very interesting and planet-conscious man. I learned that John had written a number of books inspired by the shaman's teachings, showing us a better way to live. He also spoke of a grassroots movement called Dream Change Coalition which later became known as Dream Change. It includes many people from many cultures and inspires us to be more aware of our earth. He then went on to mention a workshop he gives to help others learn to apply the ways of the indigenous cultures to our everyday lives. He called this workshop "Shapeshifting." It sounded very interesting even though I had a hard time imagining what it would be like to attend one of his workshops. I never considered myself tuned in to indigenous cultures, although speaking an Amazonian language proved otherwise.

Patience, persistence and faith had finally paid off. By the time our conversation ended, he assured me once again he would send my tape to his friend, Ipupiara. He said he would then have Ipupiara get in touch with me at a later date. John inspired confidence that the foreign words flowing through my voice held real meaning, which was validating to me. Of course being in a state of shock it never occurred to me to ask more questions. I just scribbled down everything he was saying as best and as fast as I possibly could on an envelope I had grabbed nearby.

Sitting there, still holding the phone in one hand and a pen in the other, I could hardly believe what just took place. Laughing and crying simultaneously, I felt exhilarated. I just found out something concrete about the language I was speaking. It is real, it does exist—I knew it! I was so pumped I immediately called Carl at work. Of all the times I've called him in the past, this was the one time he couldn't be reached. I hung up and dialed Debbie's number. She has been through this with me since the beginning and I couldn't wait to tell her!

"Hello," a sleepily voice answered.

"Debbie?" I practically yelled.

"Uh huh, what's up?" She asked.

"I'm sorry, did I wake you up?" I said nervously.

"Yeah, that's okay, what's up?"

"You're not going to believe this—I just hung up from talking to John Perkins. He told me he believes I'm speaking an indigenous Amazonian language. Can you believe it?" I rattled on, sharing some inconsequential thoughts. "I'm sorry I called so early, but I had to tell you. Isn't that wild?"

"That's great Janet, I'm glad you finally found someone who knows what it is."

"I know, I can't believe it, it finally happened. I have an answer. Oh no, it's getting late, I gotta get to work, I'll call you back later, okay?"

"Okay, and congratulations," Debbie said.

"Thanks, love ya, bye," and I hung up quickly.

Wow, it was indeed a real language. It had a destination, an origin. It was amazing to think about. I would never have imagined in a million years that I'd be in this situation. Wow, who would have thought—as a child raised Catholic, who became a wife and mother—as a professional floral designer, become psychic medium confronting death issues—now the speaker of an Amazonian tribal language. Quite a mixed bag, and a little unconventional wouldn't you agree? Isn't expanding our journey with new experiences what life is all about? Unconventional doesn't seem like such a bad thing if looked at in that perspective. My next step would be waiting to hear from Ipupiara. Until then, I'd have to be satisfied with knowing that I spoke an actual language.

I found myself in new territory. I knew zilch about the Amazon or its people, except they lived in an exotic rain forest. I decided in the weeks that followed to get on the Internet and learn what I could about indigenous people of the Amazon. Finding articles wasn't as easy as I first thought, but when I did find them, they were eye-openers. Their culture was so foreign to mine, and extremely fascinating. I felt like I have been living in a bubble. It seems from what I read that many of the tribes had little contact with the outside world. I had a hard time imagining this contrast with my own life. They live completely off the land as their ancestors have done for thousands of years. Food, shelter, and clothing all come from knowledge passed down from the voices of generations past. They barter and fight with other tribes for what they want and need. They also heal using Shamans, herbs and plants. Worlds away, I at first began to think they were far, far behind our modern world, but I had to stop and check my beliefs. Negatively judging a culture because they don't have iPods and cell phones, doesn't make their culture primitive—quite the opposite in my opinion. They have Shamans that understand the medicinal use of plants, something our pharmaceutical companies have also learned to do. They honor Earth far more than most of us, including myself. I began to wonder how I fit into this equation. I wasn't sure, but I knew I had to walk this path, wherever it may lead me.

After a number of weeks contemplating whether or not to journey even farther out of my box, I decided to attend one of John Perkin's Shapeshifting seminars. The closest one to Missouri was in Michigan, and I called the retreat location and made reservations. The seminar was three months away and by the time the weekend approached, I was ready for my new experience. Carl and Matt were going to have a father/son weekend and watch the hot-air balloon race at Forest Park while I was away. It is a blessing that Carl has given me such unbelievable support through this entire journey. The fact he didn't question my desire to attend a seminar named "Shapeshifting" says a lot. I can't imagine many husbands supporting this roller coaster ride of life I've been on. He has trusted me, in what I need to do, never once telling me I was crazy or needed therapy. Whether he thought it, is beside the point. Like an unsolved mystery, Carl wanted me to find the answers that plagued my visions and the translation of the words that flowed through my voice as much as I did. I'm thankful that he is the man he is.

I left a day early so I could visit my younger brother Jim, who lived in Chicago. We enjoyed dinner at a Chicago favorite and spent the evening talking about my trip, my language and catching up on family news. I brought him a box of goodies just like I used to do when he was in college, so he picked through that as we chatted the night away. Hanging out with my brother was a great way to start a memorable weekend.

As Friday morning arrived, my brother headed off to work and I continued my journey to the retreat center. I left extra early to make sure I was on time, since I despise being late. Arriving even earlier than planned, I decided to head to the only store in town for Kleenex and junk food. Walking through the aisle I was surprised when I passed a man who looked vaguely familiar, but I couldn't place him. Realization dawned, it was John Perkins. I remember seeing his 1" x 3" picture on the back of his book. I chose not to introduce myself, deciding to wait until I got to the retreat. I didn't think he needed someone cornering him like a celebrity at the grocery store. Although I probably should have said something, I'm a little shy at first introductions, so I waited. Besides, I would see him soon enough.

After throwing the Kleenex, Nacho Cheese Bugles and Hostess Powdered Donuts onto the passenger seat, I drove toward the retreat center, passing scenic areas of untamed woodland. Swaying to nature's tune, the tall grasses danced in the wind. I arrived to see an area of untouched beauty laid out before me. Traveling down the narrow matted dirt and grass road avoiding the uneven dips and jutting rocks, I glanced around and stopped to gaze at the trees. Their branches were twisted, entangled in crisscrossing patterns, entwined with each other along the road. The backdrop held a cerulean blue sky swirling with white like a creation on a painter's palette.

I couldn't believe the journey I was on. I've seen visions no one would ever want to see, many times wanting to hide from them forever. I've read about people who had visions similar to mine, with the exception of the advance death notices. I wonder how they dealt with it. Since the language emerged, my focus at least has changed in that the visions seem to be few and far between. During this weekend I was hoping to learn to apply and understand some of the techniques used to bring intrapersonal change. I began to quickly identify with this intensive and experimental approach, which would give me the tools to improve clarity and become more focused. I wanted more than anything to "Shed barriers of fear," which was a line that resonated deep within. I was ready to *Shapeshift*.

John Perkins created a beautiful learning experience. As a group we learned experimental hands-on techniques for change on cellular and personal levels. Connecting with our Spirit guides, materializing dreams, awakening our subconscious source of energy, creativity and strength are all possibilities for enhancing our life's journey.

It was during the afternoon break on Saturday that I finally approached John to thank him for listening to my tape and sending it to his friend. He asked if I would be willing to share my story with the others. I was apprehensive as first after everything I've been though in the past, but forced myself to say, "I'd love to." He provided me with an opportunity to share my story with a group I discovered were open minded. His encouragement propelled me to face my fear of rejection. I realized as I began it didn't matter anymore what anyone thought, I needed to stay true to myself. With curious people surrounding me, I spoke the Amazonian language. The words glided off my tongue, my voice strong, my hands slowly moving with the gentle grace of Spirit, speaking their own unique language. I felt the message that was coming through reach out and touch each person in the room. Traveling to each individual, my eyes made contact as if to emphasize a message, unknown words somehow specific just for them. It didn't matter at that time what was being said. I could feel the powerful energy move through me and it felt electrified as if Spirit was using me as a conduit to share this gift with each human being present that day. As I spoke I felt my energy connect with theirs as if lightning shot from my soul to electrify whomever I glanced upon. Winding down, I looked to the side where John had been standing and he smiled. As he walked to the front of the room he voiced that he thought the message was a blessing. He recognized some of the words, and it was a blessing from Spirit. I was honored, and also ecstatic he knew bits and pieces of what I'd spoken.

Afterwards, many approached me with positive and warm responses offering me best wishes on my future journey. Some asked me to speak it again and so I did. We just sat around and enjoyed the break. As the evening approached a Fire Ceremony was performed for those who wished to attend. It was transcending. Being exposed to a sacred ceremonial cleansing, transforming the soul under the starry sky, a fierce bonfire cracking and absorbing the energy we shed, was emotional. As if awakening a new self, one of discovery and healing, I felt empowered. The weekend was very transformational for me, as well as spiritual. Although I knew we humans have so much more within us to offer, John Perkins helped me realize that I can expand my beliefs, find answers within and stay true to myself at the same time. I became more comfortable talking about my language with others. It no longer seemed to matter what they thought. It simply exists, period.

I returned home to find an email from John. He asked if his friend Ipupiara, to whom he sent my tape, had contacted me over the past weekend. I replied that he hadn't. His email contained Ipupiara's email address and he suggested I contact him. It was now time to see what monumental revelation the language bestowed upon me. I pulled up an email and began typing. Stopping often to reword a sentence, I read it, did a quick spell check and with the click of the mouse, off it went, through cyberspace and on to Ipupiara.

Chapter Six

Sacred Earth

The limits of my language mean the limits of my world.
Ludwig Wittgenstein

Ipupiara replied to my email with his phone number and informed me when he would be available. The moment of truth was about to arrive. Four years of anticipation and waiting seemed to be heading toward a final climax. The few days leading up to the call, left me nervous and pacing, my thoughts fully occupied. I was consumed by the multiple questions filtering through my mind: What is the name of the language I'm speaking? Did he get my tape translated? What does it say? What is he like? Will he continue to help me translate more tapes? Will there be others to assist me? The list in my mind snowballed down a steep hill only to shoot up a steep crest where it sat waiting in massive proportion teetering on the edge. Finally, there was only one more day to go, and although close, each second ticked by slowly.

Sunday afternoon finally arrived. Ironic I thought, remembering this language first emerged on a Sunday afternoon and here it is another Sunday, over four years later. I was looking forward to understanding more about this language and getting some much needed answers. Sitting in the kitchen, a room full of comfort and warmth, I shakily poured myself a cup of decaffeinated coffee in one of the hand-crafted pottery mugs I collect, and tried to relax. I dialed Ipupiara's phone number.

"Hello, may I please speak with Ipupiara?" I asked, my voice cracking.

"Yes, this is Ipupiara," he replied.

"Hi, this is Janet. John Perkins sent you my tape."

"Yes, Yes, Janet. I have the tape. Can I ask you to explain how you came to speak this language?"

"Sure," I said and I recounted my story as if reciting a play committed to memory from telling the story so many times.

When I finished Ipupiara stated, "Janet, I have a hard time believing this. I have never heard of something like this happening. I listen to the tape and know it's true, but continue to wrestle with the possibility."

"I understand Ipupiara, it does seem like the impossible, but I can tell you, it's possible."

"May I ask you some questions?" he asked inquisitively.

"Sure, ask away!" I openly replied.

"They may get personal," he stated.

"Um, okay," I said, wondering what he could possibly ask me that would relate to the language and be personal at the same time.

"Have you ever traveled to South America?"

"No," I replied, "Actually, I've never been outside of the United States."

He then asked: "Have you ever taken hallucinogenic drugs?"

I started laughing and then I realized he was serious and I said, "No, I don't do drugs of any kind." I did explain how I have asthma and I take medication for that. That is the extent of my drug usage.

"Have you ever drank Ayahuasca?"

"I have no idea what Aya.., how did you say that again?" I questioned.

"Ayahuasca."

"And what is it and why do you drink it?" I asked.

"Ayahuasca is a hallucinogenic substance from a plant in South America. It is only used for tribal ceremonies to gain spiritual connections with the Spirit world. It brings inner healing and knowledge."

"I can definitely say I have never had that before!" I stated emphatically. "It seems I'm already trying to achieve that on my own without the Ayahuasca."

"Janet, is there someone you know who speaks this language?" Ipupiara asked.

"Besides you?" I laughed. "No, I know of no one who speaks this, that's why I've spent four and a half years searching for someone who does. Although, I wish I had, it sure would have made life a lot easier for me over the years."

"I see. Do you have any medical problems?" he wanted to know next.

I mentioned again, "I have asthma and use an inhaler, but that's it."

Slowly, as if choosing his wording carefully, he asked, "Are there any other medical conditions or issues?"

I suddenly realized he was cautiously asking me if I had any mental problems.

"No, only what I told you about my story of the visions I have," I answered.

"You take no other medications Janet?" he asked.

"Nope, just my inhaler for asthma," I said.

"Can you say something in Yanomami for me Janet?" he asked.

"Is that what I'm speaking? Yanomami?" I questioned excitedly.

"Yes," Ipupiara answered. "Can you speak something for me now?"

"I would be happy to," I exclaimed, thinking how cool it was that I could finally put a name to this beautiful language coming through me.

I began speaking it quickly and then it just stopped as if a statement had been made.

"Do you know what you just said?" Ipupiara asked.

"No, do you know what I said?" I asked a little impatiently.

"Yes."

After a long pause, feeling like the snowball fell off the ridge and landed on my head, I asked, "Well?"

"You were speaking of the Fierce People. This is what the Yanomami people are called. The Fierce People." Ipupiara explained.

"Could you spell the name for me?"

"Janet sweetie woman, there are many spellings that are close to this language and a number of tribes as well. I will give you one. Y-A-N-O-M-A-M-I."

"Thank you Ipupiara. It's nice to finally put a name to the language I am speaking." I admitted.

"Can you say something else?" Ipupiara asked.

"Sure," and I quickly rattled off another combination of phrases and then stopped.

"Do you know what you just said?" Ipupiara asked again.

"No," I said, thinking to myself, *haven't we been through this already?* "Can you tell me what I just said?" I asked again.

"You were talking about the White People. This is what they call themselves when they pray."

"Oh wow, that's pretty cool," I said.

"Janet, you speak this well, I am surprised by this."

I didn't really know what to say to that so I asked instead, "Ipupiara, why do you think I am speaking this. Why me?"

"Why not?" he said.

And so, our first conversation was more like "twenty questions" than anything else. At times it felt like the "Who's on First" Abbott and Costello Skit. All humor aside, I could tell Ipupiara was very cautious in his questioning. It's no stretch that he would wonder how this happened. He mentioned he knew some of the Yanomami people and spoke some of their dialects. Understandable, considering he shared with me that he is an indigenous South America shaman. He was born into the Uru-e Wau Wau tribe in northern Brazil, near the Venezuelan border. The name of his tribe translates as "People of the Stars." Although I learned little at the time, I later found out he attended school under the name Bernardo Peixoto to learn the North American ways and received his Ph. D. in Anthropology and Biology so he could help bridge his South American culture and North American culture. Ipupiara informed me he knows languages of Peru and Brazil, (Quechua and Tupi) and many other dialects as well. Luckily for me, he happened to know the one I was speaking. He explained he would translate the entire tape and then get back to me. As of yet, he had only listened to it a couple of times and made some notes. Traveling extensively as he did, he informed me it may take a while before he could get back to me. I had no problem with that at all. If he was offering to translate the tape, I wouldn't complain.

I was told he works at the Smithsonian Institute teaching classes on South American culture and the healing powers of plants. He is a consultant to the National Zoo and in the past he has been an advisor to the White House. It seems I just added to his many duties.

Heck with the coffee, I was going to celebrate with a glass of wine! Ecstatic to know and have a translator, it was clearly a day for celebration. He promised as time allowed he would get back to me. As much as I wanted to demand he translate the tape immediately, I knew instead I must wait patiently being satisfied with whatever could be offered. For now, I was content with having a name for this language that comes through with such elegant energy.

Yanomami-it even sounded like an exotic indigenous name. This language, flowing through my voice, finally has a name.

Yanomami...I could say it all day long.

And so our unique and unusual relationship began.

A couple months after our first conversation, Ipupiara called me back.

"Hello Janet, how are you?" He asked.

"I'm great Ipupiara and you?"

"I'm good. I'm sorry it took me a while to get back to you, but I've been busy."

"No problem." I said with palpable excitement.

"So Janet, are you ready to hear what is on the tape?"

"Yes! I've been waiting for four and a half years Ipupiara. I'm almost shaking, no, I am shaking, I'm so excited. I almost can't believe this moment has finally arrived."

"Janet, do you have pen and paper?" he asked.

"Yes I do and I'm all ready to go Ipupiara." I stated.

"Good, and call me Ipu, all my friends do."

"Okay, Ipu."

"Janet, this tape John mailed to me was sixty minutes long. It took many hours to translate it. I was surprised by what was said and for a number of reasons. First, the Yanomami Spirit who came through voiced that..."

PART III

The Tapes and The Messages They Leave Behind

"My voice is one of many."

The First Tape

"Be Earth-Honoring"

"We need to be more Earth-Honoring People," Ipu replied.

That's it? I waited over four and a half years to hear that? I was a little disappointed. I was thinking something more along the lines of, "I am here to share the secrets to the universe—or maybe, I've bestowed this gift of enlightenment upon you because you're such a wonderful person." Okay, so maybe not exactly that, but this spirit came through simply to tell me and anyone who's listening to be more earth-honoring? Does this mean I have to toss the paper plates? The Styrofoam cups? Start planting vegetables? Heck, I don't even like vegetables, I'd be happy to toss those. I realized I hadn't replied to Ipu's translation and so I repeated,

"We need to be more earth-honoring people?"

"Yes Janet, and the message is repeated *twenty-three times,*" Ipu stated.

"That's interesting since twenty-three is my favorite number," I commented without thinking as I scribbled it down.

"There is more," he said.

"Oh good," I said, thinking, here comes the good stuff.

"Are you ready?" Ipu asked.

"Yes!" I said impatiently.

"Messages will be released: Honor Fire, Water, Air, Mother Earth."

"Okay," I said as I wrote down the words, once again a bit disappointed.

"This message was repeated *seventeen times,*" Ipu stated.

"Seventeen, okay, anything else?" I questioned.

"Yes and this I found surprising, you were speaking in the male dialect," Ipu commented.

"How do you know that?" I asked.

"Because some of the words are taboo for the woman to speak and since you were speaking them, the spirit coming through you would have to be male," Ipu shared.

"Wow, well, that is bizarre," I said. "So, you're telling me a male spirit is speaking through me?"

"I'm not sure how this is happening, but yes, it would seem so," he replied.

"Ok, but could I have been reincarnated and maybe was a Yanomami male in a past life?" I asked.

"I don't know and this tape doesn't say. So until we know more I can't guess," Ipu said.

"Yeah, your right. I was just curious," I replied. "Kind of wild I was saying words that are taboo for the woman to speak," I added.

"Yes, I was surprised by this as well," Ipu chimed in.

"Okay so go on, what else was said?" I inquired.

"Well some of what you said was a type of prayer, but I couldn't understand it. Only a few words. The words didn't come through very clearly, but you spoke of healing Mother Earth and it sounded like a chant. Parts of the tape were difficult to understand," he expressed.

"I guess when you think about it, I can understand why," I said.

"So, what else?" I inquired.

"That's it, Janet," he said.

"That's it?" I asked a bit loudly.

That's all that was said in a sixty minute tape? I thought to myself.

"Janet, you were talking very slowly and they repeated the messages numerous times."

"Yeah, you're right Ipu. I'm sorry. I guess I didn't really think about it," I muttered.

"Janet, I want you to make another tape and send it to me," Ipu requested.

"I would be happy too. I'll make one right away," I said.

"Take your time. It's going to be awhile before I can translate it and that takes days as well."

"Okay, Ipu thanks so much for sharing this with me and taking all the time to translate it. I hope you know I really appreciate it."

"You're welcome, Janet. You have very important messages here that need to be shared," he said.

"You think so?" I questioned a bit surprisingly.

"Yes, if this spirit is sending you a message telling you and those on the planet to be more earth-honoring, then he must feel the message needs to be spoken."

"Good point," I said.

"Think about this, you have been chosen to get these messages out. There must be a reason why you were selected," Ipu stated.

"I guess, I'm just worried this spirit accidentally dropped into the wrong body!" I said jokingly, but wondered all along if that might be the case.

"I need to be going, so you take care Janet and blessings."

"Thanks Ipu, blessings to you too."

Hanging up the phone, I sat there staring at what was written before me. Realizing I was over my disappointment about receiving a so-called enlightened message, it hit me in many ways I HAD received just that. It was just so much bigger than me, it was global. I had never thought on that scale before. Wow, what am I supposed to do now? I can't see myself passing flyers around proclaiming: We need to be more Earth-honoring people. I guess I could share the message with those I know or come into contact with, then perhaps work my way up? This was no longer just about me—it includes everyone inhabiting our planet. I think I was just given another job to do. Would this be considered global marketing? The world was a little more than I was planning to take on. My road to personal enlightenment was beginning to look like a steep hill going straight up with lots of rocks, something I wasn't going to be able to climb easily. I hope this didn't mean the funds in my Karma bank were getting low because I'd like to think that was one bank account I contributed to daily. I wondered what words of enlightened wisdom were going to emerge next time.

The Second Tape
"Fulnio"

When Ipu called this time, I was prepared to have no personal expectations. No matter what came through, I was going to listen with an open mind and an open heart. If I was chosen to get these messages out to the world, then I better chuck my personal agenda and listen instead.

"Hi Ipu, it's been a while, how are you?"

"Good Janet, I have the translation of this tape and it seems we have another surprise."

"Really? What is it," I asked.

"Let me explain. This tape continued from the first tape in Yanomami with the exact same message."

"Ipu, how is that possible? The last tape was probably six months old, maybe more," I said.

"It is the same message, to be more Earth-honoring and repeated many times as well. However, a second language emerged part way through. You repeat the same message, only in a different language. It is somewhat similar, called Fulnio."

"Wow, that's wild," I said.

"There's more, in this language, you are female."

"How do you know?" I asked.

"Because certain words are used or maybe I should say not used. That is the best way I can explain it," Ipu replied.

"Okay. So anything else?" I questioned.

"Yes, the female spirit says to, *Hear this!*" with emphasis.

"*That people from the four corners of the world will come to hear the prophecy.*"

"That sounds pretty big to me," I remarked.

"Yes, and then she continues by saying, *the messages will be released, the messages will be released.* It is a very powerful tape Janet, and it says one last thing," Ipu exclaimed.

"What?" I asked.

"This female spirit who comes through says to: *make offering to Mother Earth, plant in her womb. Items such as corn, cotton, bananas.* And she goes on to say: *Very powerful moments are coming. Evil will disappear soon and Mother Earth will have to be appeased,*" Ipu explained.

"That sounds promising," I stated.

"She ends the tape by saying: *Be Earth-honoring.*"

"Sounds like we need to take care of our planet."

"Yes, we do."

"Well Ipu, I don't know what to think about this one."

"Janet, it seems there are multiple messages going on here, as if you have a number of Spirits speaking through you."

"I guess when I think about it Ipu, sometimes it does seem to sound a little different. Sometimes it may come through really forceful, then other times it's quieter or more contemplative. I'll have to pay closer attention. I wonder if I would be able to sense if the energy is male or female."

"Janet, you need to get these messages out."

"Yeah I know, I'll have to think about how I'm going to accomplish that," I said.

"Well, I'm very busy at this time, but make another tape and we'll see what comes through," Ipu said.

"Okay, sounds great and hey, thanks Ipu. I really appreciate your help and your time."

"Your welcome, sweetie, take care," and he hung up.

I didn't really know what to think of this tape, except it was a surprise as Ipu stated. So, now, male and female spirits were speaking through me. This was in a way another affirmation via another avenue that confirms when we die, we continue to exist. We just don't turn to ashes and that's it. It's almost as if it was Spirit's way of reiterating the fact that what I have seen in the past does exist. Telling someone I saw a spirit of a woman is one thing. Telling them spirit has channeled their message through me in another language is more persuasive? Who knows? One thing I do know is that life isn't dull in my little corner of the world.

The Third Tape

"The Eagle and the Condor"

Once again many months passed until the next tape had been translated. Ipu was extremely busy and I was so blessed that he took time for me, I was willing to wait until whenever he was available. By now, I was learning I not only had patience, I had a lot of it. It was a good lesson.

"Hello Ipu, great to hear from you again," I said excitedly.

"Hello Janet honey, how are you?" he asked.

"I'm good, and you?" I inquired.

"Busy, very busy," he replied.

"Well, thanks for taking time to translate the tape, Ipu."

"I want to do this Janet, it just takes time. I'm sorry for the delay but I just returned from Brazil and I'll tell you about that after we speak of the tape."

"Ok, sounds good Ipu. So what does this tape have to say?" I asked excitedly.

"Janet, this tape starts where the last one left off again."

"No way! That is so bizarre! It's months in-between, how does that happen? I guess for now that's an enigma, huh?"

"Time doesn't exist to them like it does to us," he replied.

"Yeah, I've heard that before. It must be true," I commented.

"This tape speaks in both languages again and both male and female are present as well. They mention again separately, *We need to be more Earth-honoring.* Then the male goes on to say: *Moments of struggle coming up. Two groups, one will accept the prophecy, one will not. Some will listen, some will not. Two powerful people (or animals) will share knowledge.*

Ipu went on to explain this is called—*The PACHI CUTI prophecy........ The Eagle from the North and the Condor from the South will come together and share Experience and Knowledge. This will be accomplished in the coming millennium. We need to be more Earth-honoring.*

"I'm not sure I understand what the Pachi Cuti prophecy is, Ipu," I stated.

"Janet, it means the Eagle or people from the North (North America) which is power, and the Condor or people from the South (South America), which is wisdom come together, they will learn from each other gaining experience and knowledge."

"That sounds like a good idea in general Ipu," I said. "Bringing ideas from each continent to come together and gain knowledge from each other."

"Yes, this Pachi Cuti prophecy takes place every five hundred years and the time is now."

"Wow, then they have the time frame right as well," I said surprisingly.

"Yes, it is. This is very interesting Janet."

"Yeah, I agree Ipu."

"Then at the end of the tape it says: *I hope you understand what I have on here.* (Meaning on this tape)," Ipu explained.

"Hmm, I wonder what that means?" I inquired.

"I think they are trying to let us know this is important, so remember it," Ipu replied.

"Well, I'll remember, but I don't know what I can do right now," I said.

When Ipu finished giving me the translation he started to tell me about his trip to Brazil to visit with the Yanomami and Tucano people. He told me he brought one of my tapes and played it for them. They danced around the cassette player, listening and saying. "Cariuas abate inan" or "White woman speaking Yanomami." He actually had to run back to town the following day to get more batteries because they wanted to continue to listen to the message, and the tape player drained the batteries. He explained one defining moment when he first turned on the tape recorder. The women heard the words being spoken, and ran from the tape recorder. Some of the words being said were taboo for them to hear, so they were required to leave. Since I'm not familiar with their culture and beliefs, I found this fascinating. It was an empowering moment for me. Just speaking their language is enough to make me feel connected with these people.

Ipu ended with saying, "Remember, the Great Spirit is channeling through you great messages."

"Thank you Ipu, I promise to do what I can to let others know as well."

After our conversation I sat and tried to digest this translation. It spoke of prophecy. I imagine that since I am an open channel for them, they can come through with all sorts of guidance they feel is needed for our planet and to help each other. It's interesting information to think about. I liked the idea that these spirits are trying to bring the North and South together. Learning quickly its evident both sides can learn from one another.

What fascinated me even more was the fact the Yanomami people understood my tape and danced around it. How amazing would it be to actually be there and talk to them? Who knows what could happen. Then again, I don't know what I'm saying and they do carry spears and machetes. I guess I would just have to take my chances.

The Fourth Tape

"Ritual and Ceremony"

Ipu and I spent many months playing phone tag and so it was decided he would email me what he had translated from tape four. Ipu explained that what had come through was very unusual and that he was unclear about its meaning. He noted that he wanted to stay true to what he translated, so I could decide what I thought it meant. The tape again continues from tape three with the same messages, however some new information emerges.

Janet,

This is what I have translated on your fourth tape: The words: *Ritual and Ceremony* were widely used throughout the tape. The word *evil* came through as well.

Here is what was found:

Happily on this trail of positive pollen may I walk, happily may I walk.
House made of healing bricks.
With beauty I will walk and chant for hours and hours.
With beauty behind me may I walk and also heal people.
With beauty all around me may I chant and heal others.
The world of dead is returning.
The spirits brought us this message over the new earth; they are coming to talk to us.
This is what spirits have promised.

People, take this path, go this way, it is a goodly path, says the Spirit.
It leads to a joyous place, not evil.
We the Spirits are talking through a few special people.
Not all people can be the spirit road.
These messages have to be spread all over the earth.
More and more messages will be coming to people that will not be able to understand what is happening.
The Spirits need to communicate with you.
Prayer will be pronounced loud and clear to the four corners of the world.
Our message has to be heard.
The wind will also send messages.
We are all here and we will stay here as long as we need.

Ipu ends with comments that they repeat this over and over and it sounds like the Spirits are eager to communicate. He thinks it's cool and neat.

Well, that was quite a message.

For the record, I don't consider myself any more special than the next person. Each person on this planet is unique and special. This tape represents to me an awakening for everyone to take note that there is more happening around us than we realize. Never in a million years would I have imagined speaking languages I don't know or haven't studied. I'll admit, I'm pretty average. Outside of the visions and languages, I don't really stand out in any way and I'm cool with that. Yet, it seems I was given an important duty and that is to remind people to be more Earth-honoring. Possibly also to let everyone know that more channels will emerge, and I'm not talking cable channels.

I wasn't too thrilled to see the word evil in my tape. It was a little scary I'll admit. I started thinking the worst, allowing negative comments from friends and relatives to creep up in my conscious thoughts. Ipu explained that rituals and ceremonies are used to ward off evil spirits. I took this as the equivalent of praying for good over evil. If someone is ill, you pray for their recovery. I could be incorrect, but I wondered if indigenous tribes considered illness an evil? In the simplest of ways many claim that goodness could not be understood without evil. Since I've never been one to believe evil has a hold over anyone, I figured I was in good shape.

When it was mentioned about me walking on positive pollen, my first thought was allergy season and that would be springtime. It is a beautiful time of year when the flowers began to bloom, beauty is everywhere, except for where the yellow-green pollen leaves its trail of dust.

As for healing, I have taken a number of Pranic Healing courses by Master Stephen Co and Master Choa Kok Sui, but I'm not experienced enough nor have I had enough practice to assume I am in any way a professional healer. It's possible the spirits who speak through me are healers in some way. If that is the case, then they must feel they can work through me to heal. If they can manipulate my vocal cords and send energy through me to speak their language, why not send energy to heal?

This is all so new to me on so many levels, trying to understand the ways of the indigenous people and how they perceive life though the tapes. I'm so ignorant about their culture, and although I want to learn, I also feel the less I know, the better. This way knowing as little as possible won't cloud what does comes through. Whether knowing more or less is even an issue, I haven't a clue. This is a long way away from making peanut butter and jelly sandwiches every morning for my son's lunch or dropping off kids in carpool. Even a long way from being a floral designer.

I also took note about messages coming from the winds. To me it feels like they are talking about earth changes, but again, I could be incorrect. Everyone has their own interpretation and maybe that is the way it should be. Then what is said cannot be clouded by any perception or judgment. Maybe someone out there has my answers.

The Fifth Tape
"The Poem"

"Hello Janet, how are you?" Ipu inquired.

"Ipu! It's great to hear from you. I'm great and you?" I asked.

"Doing good, busy too. I have tape five Janet and it's very interesting. It sounds like the spirit is sharing a poem."

"A poem? That's odd," I replied.

"Yes, let me read it to you, you have pen and paper?" he asked.

"Yes, I do, go ahead."

"It begins with, '*This, the language of wisdom.*'"

"Wait, wait a minute, what did you just say?" I asked as my memory leapt back to months earlier. A chill ran down my spine. "Could you repeat that again?"

"It begins with, *This, the language of wisdom.*"

"Oh my God, Ipu! Hold on, Okay?" I started to shake. "I know I wrote a poem months before starting with that exact sentence or at least similar. Hold on a sec Ipu, let me go find it and read mine first. This is so wild, I'll be right back," I said as I put down the phone and ran to the closet, grabbed the backpack and scurried through it to find the poem I knew was in there. A flashback from months earlier emerged.

I awoke one summer morning with the intense compulsion to write. Time was not on my side. My son's swim lesson was within the hour. Grabbing a pen and pad of paper, it got tossed in a backpack with Matt's towel and sunscreen. We arrived for his lesson and he walked over to his instructor, near the pool's edge, and jumped in. Seeing he was settled, I sat down to write. This sudden obsession I awoke with was propelling me to put pen to paper immediately. I began tossing words down from thoughts and feeling and my hand moved as if guided by an outside source. An occasional glance toward my son as the sun shimmered across the water made me smile. The voices of the children's laughter and their splashes faded around me as I continued to write. What emerged was a poem that bridges humanity, earth and spirit. Completing the spontaneous poem, I was left with a sense of accomplishment that whatever or whoever prompted me to write was satisfied. I was. Matt's swim lesson came to an end so I quickly gathered up my stuff, paraded over to Matt with a big smile and headed out. As the day turned hectic, the poem lay forgotten in the backpack with the sunscreen.

I now pulled it out, ran back into the kitchen and grabbed the phone. "Ok, here it is," I said breathlessly as I read him my poem first.

This Language of Wisdom

When I speak this loving language
My heart opens from within
I am guided through the beauty of the rainforest
I feel the waves gently roll in from the sea
I am a flower blooming before the sunlight
I am a melody of human tissue
I am a Soul of this Spirit's Blessings
When I speak this loving language
I am old, I am new
My ancient life mingles with the now
I am all things, I am nothing
There is sunshine
There is rain that speaks through my soul
I am human, I am so much more
I am here and Yet, I am there
I live in two worlds
I am on a journey of this soul
I journey for planet's peace
Blessings!

When I finished he said, "Janet, it is very similar. Let me read this to you."

This is the translation he conveyed:

This, the language of Wisdom
Language that I love
You are part of my soul
This language lives inside of me
Wisdom, Wisdom, Wisdom
This language sounds like a melody
This will be my long journey
A journey to the spirits
I feel so good, so parallel with the worlds and reality
I'm Pacha Mama
I am so much more
Rain drops to fertilize the hearts of people who listen to this
When I speak this language I am ancient
I trust in the power and path I am trying to walk through
I learn to forgive myself and others
I remember how many mistakes I make
This is the healing message that comes from somewhere
A feeling in my heart, a cold breeze
Help Me, Help me Pacha Mama

"Wow, Ipu that is pretty similar," I said.

"Yes Janet, it is."

"I remember the day I wrote that, how I was almost obsessed wanting to write something."

"What do you think that means?" I asked.

"Maybe spirit is telling you that you can communicate with them in many ways."

"Wow, I don't know what to think. Maybe I can understand them in some ways after all, huh?" I said.

"Janet, you need to continue to work with these spirits when they want to come through."

"I thought I was, Ipu," I stated, "but when they spontaneously propel through me when I'm grocery shopping or working or wherever I may be, it's inappropriate. This may sound crazy, but I've had to ask them to not spontaneously come through unless it's important, promising to work with them if they stop popping through at inappropriate moments. It has seemed to work. Maybe now they are letting me know they can work with me while writing too."

"Yes Janet, try to stay open to them, and continue to channel their great messages."

"Okay Ipu, thanks," I said contemplatively.

"Your welcome Janet, have a blessed day."

"Thanks and you do the same."

This tape really made me realize so much more is going on than I can comprehend. Emotional, I wondered if it was time to re-define what being human meant. Somewhere along the line, the Yanomami language crossed over to my thoughts in English. So, were they my thoughts? Theirs? Both? It was pretty wild and at the same time eerie. Am I allowing them to think for me or am I simply the channel from which they broadcast? It was my misfortune there was no one to call and voice my concerns. I was left to my own devices. Most days, having this opportunity to speak the language was such a beautiful gift. However, some days it was a bit like living in a sci-fi movie, never being sure what was going to happen around the next corner. I guess when the time comes and I wake up on the other side, I'm going to have a lot of questions, even more than the average person. Then again, maybe I'll already know the answers by then.

The Video
"Prayer for the Dead"

Ipu asked me if I would be willing to make a video tape speaking in Yanomami and/or Fulnio, whichever came through. Since I wasn't exactly video savvy I had Carl set the video recorder up and I sat at the kitchen table and gave a short message. The video was then sent off to Ipu. He called me months down the road and asked:

"Janet, who was holding the video camera?"
I had to think about it and I answered, "No one, why?"
"Because what you spoke of was a *prayer for the dead* and I wondered if the person holding the camera died since you sent this."
Man, that was freaky, I thought to myself, but then went on to say, "Actually, at the time I was thinking of my Uncle Paul who had died, wondering if he was on the other side watching out for my relatives and me."
"Was anyone holding the camera?" Ipu asked again impatiently.
"No, actually Carl propped it up on some books on the ironing board," all the while embarrassed thinking, "*classy,* I know." "I even gave him trouble about the homemade tripod he rigged up, at least they didn't talk about that."
"Okay then, I'm just making sure," he said.

When we disconnected, I wondered what the words were for the *prayer for the dead,* but Ipu didn't elaborate. We never seemed to have enough time on the phone and I always thought, I'll ask next time, only to move on to the next situation that always arose.

The Sixth Tape
"Release the Messages"

Ipu and I once again spent many months playing phone tag and so he decided to just email me what he had translated from tape six. It was unusual and unique, as they all seemed to be. He didn't want to make any assumptions, only stay true to what he translated. I could decide what I thought it meant.

Janet,

This is what I have translated on your sixth tape:

You are a teacher, such a powerful master. Don't chase it away, go to it beloved one.
Don't be shy, your spirit adjusts yourself to your powerful energy.
Now come to the end of the 27 mountains, 27 ridges.
It wounds your heart, it troubles him.
I undress to your face and I show my nakedness, this power is mine.
I am the channel, come to me, steer down toward me.
Come to me up here in the coolness.
Welcome supernatural one, we have come to meet alive, long-live-makers.

Yeah, I pretty much thought the same thing, "Wow, I'm clueless here."

I began to break it down, and it soon began to flow and make sense in a comforting way. One main point I gleaned from this was that possibly I needed to embrace my energy. If my nakedness was to put myself out there before the world, as in exposing oneself then they were telling me to go ahead. They were exposing themselves as well to me. The channeling, I would agree, is the connection I have with spirit, I'm a channel or vessel for spirit to work through.

Maybe when this life is through, we'll meet again, on the other side *alive* as mentioned, just as we are meeting alive here. It was encouraging to be reminded, although we shed our bodies, our spirits still exist and that is how they work through me.

The next section was of a more personal nature specifically directed toward me, but I am choosing to share this part in a general sense, hoping to inspire all.

The language of the spirit that speaks through me voices that- *I am channeling and connecting with the Spirit world.*
Let it flow and not stop it.
It is important for the energy to get out.
It is a reminder that- *I (we) have something important going on here and I need to be aware of it.*
It seems I am constantly reminded of this. There is constant repetition. Everything, school, work, sports, or spiritual matters, repetition is important.
The Spirits speak:
This is sacred and the messages are needed to be released.
Release the messages to others, feel their presence.

It was also mentioned that using feathers is very powerful and will allow the spirits to come through clearer. Interestingly enough, I have always loved feathers and have them displayed throughout my home. They were even placed on a hand-crafted drum that was given to me as a gift. When a sacred feather ceremony was given to me in this tape, I thought to share it with the readers. I was planning to explain what to do and how to create this ceremony. Amazingly, each time I have tried to type out the ceremony my computer suddenly has problems and shuts down or I lose the work I just typed out. I have been extremely frustrated rewriting this story multiple times. After the third incident, it dawned on me: I'm not supposed to share this one. Therefore, I'll honor this lesson from spirit and keep it to myself.

Ipu also surprised me once by asking, "Janet do you draw?"
"A little, mostly I doodle when talking on the phone, why?" I asked.
"I want you to send me these doodles."
"Why?" I asked again laughing this time.
"I want to see if you're drawing anything that is of importance to the Yanomami or Fulnio tribes."
"Okay," I remarked, thinking how odd of a request that was. "Keep in mind, they are doodles Ipu."
"I will, I'm just thinking how the spirits mentioned you'll be channeling in many ways."
"Oh, so you think they may be drawing through me, that's cool," I said. "I'll make copies and then send them."
"Thank you," Ipu replied.

After receiving the doodled artwork, Ipu called stating they were in fact meaningful. What seemed insignificant and a simple nervous habit was a hidden yet obvious message channeled through my hand, while I wasn't paying attention. Ipu said they were drawings of plants in the rainforest and symbols they use to communicate with each other. The open heart design with the spiral plant emerging out of it that you see at the beginning of each chapter is one of those "doodles." There is a part of me that finds this somewhat bizarre although not surprising—on the other hand I hold a pretty cool tool to the unknown. Hands down, spirit is good at using any outlet available.

The Seventh Tape

The "Bleedy" Tape

You have to take the bad with the good in life, and this next tape was an example of the former. Of all the tapes so far, this was the first one that spoke of mass destruction. Ipu and a Yanomami friend of his who helped him translate this tape both called it the "Bleedy" tape. Not something I found encouraging, to say the least.

"Janet, hello honey."

"Hi Ipu, it's been a while, how are ya?" I asked.

"Busy, busy as usual. Janet this tape is not a good one," he said.

"What do you mean by not a good one?" I inquired.

"It's what my friend and I call the "Bleedy" tape. It's all about destruction, floods, earth that quakes. It talks about bleedy things and speaks of pain, screaming and weeping. It's a tape of prophecy, Janet."

"That's creepy, Ipu. I don't like hearing this," I said with disappointment.

"It looks like the year 2001 is going to be a difficult one," he said.

"Well, I don't think I'll tell anyone about this one, it's scary," I proclaimed.

"Janet, you have to share all messages whether they are good or not," Ipu said wisely.

"Maybe, maybe not, I'll think about it."

"Janet, the spirits are preparing us for many changes, you must share their words."

"Okay Ipu, I'll take that into consideration," I said.

When I hung up the phone I wanted to toss that tape out the window and act like it never happened. I didn't want a negative tape. I just wanted to live in my rose-colored-spiritual-glasses world. That wasn't to be. I had to accept that life was full of changes and this was just one of those situations I would have to deal with.

The Eighth Tape
"Words of a Shaman"

The last message I made was sent to Ipu via CD. He wanted to bring my CD to the rainforest. Ipu explained that the Yanomami people and those from various other tribes traveled days to meet him. When he played the CD he informed me that it sounded differently than the others and thought I was possibly speaking yet another language. I wasn't surprised. Especially after learning the year before that a tape I sent him on his birthday came through in the Tucano language, which is similar to his own tribe's language. Hearing there may be a fourth one only made me smile.

"Janet honey, how are you?" Ipu always asked.

"I'm good Ipu, and you?" I inquired back.

"Good, busy as usual. Janet, I went to Brazil and took your CD with me."

"Oh that's great Ipu, what did you learn this time?"

"Well Janet, I played it for the chiefs of the tribes, when the female of the tribe started to hear it, she ran away and called for all the woman to go with her."

"Really? Again? Didn't that happen with the second or third tape?" I asked.

"Yes, because the words were again taboo for the woman to hear."

"Oh!"

"And the chief of the tribe said he cannot tell me what is being said."

"Why not?" I questioned.

"Because they are sacred words. Words a Shaman would use during a ceremony."

"So then, I'll never know?"

"Well, the chief said if you come to him, he will tell you what is said. He told me he can only share the message with the channel who spoke it."

"Meaning me, is that it?"

"Yes, Janet, I am sorry," Ipu replied.

"Well Ipu, you don't have to be sorry, I'm grateful for everything you have done for me."

"Well, Janet, we won't know what is on the CD unless you go to the rainforest. Then you will find out."

Laughingly, I replied, "Someday I would love to Ipu, but I guess until then, we'll just have to wait."

"One more thing Janet," he said.

"Yes?"

"You were speaking in another language. It is Canamari."

"Say that again please?"

"Canamari."

"That sounds really beautiful, Ipu."

"Yes and you were speaking a scared ceremony in Canamari, a healing ceremony as if from one Shaman to another. That is what I have been told."

"Well, that's pretty cool."

"Yes it is Janet. Maybe soon you can go to the rainforest," replied Ipu.

"Maybe Ipu, hopefully someday," I replied.

I thought about that conversation wondering what was being said, from one Shaman to the other? Wow, totally awesome—I was a channel for a Shaman Spirit. What an honor. Yet to have a Shaman speak through me is a little surreal. I often wondered if I'd wake up and realize this was all a dream. Who decides what is real anyway? Maybe that's what life is, one big dream until we awake on the other side alive, ready to share our adventure with loved ones as they gather around to hear our stories.

PART IV

Life Blessings with Spirit

Chapter Seven

Patience at Work

The events in our lives happen in a sequence in time, but in their significance to ourselves they find their own order: the continuous thread of revelation.
Eudora Welty

Reading the eight tapes in succession gives you the full impact of the channeled messages. Now, let's backtrack a bit so I can take you on a simultaneous journey I was traveling and share another amazing discovery that happened along the way. This story began at the time I was recording Tape Six.

March 2000 ... My introduction to Gary and meeting Susy

For years, Ipu assisted me through my journey despite his busy work and travel schedule, and I was constantly aware that I was asking a lot from him. Ipu is an extraordinary human being, and it's an honor and privilege to know him. He has shared with me so much of his knowledge and time, and has bridged a gap for me, a language barrier I could not have crossed on my own. He has been a true gift and a blessing. Our long-distance relationship continues, yet I wanted and needed, to discover more—if Ipu recognized these languages, then other people would too. If so, multiple tapes and messages could be shared. It's evident these messages in their simplicity hold powerful words of wisdom. I dream of someday traveling to the South American rainforest to meet these indigenous people whose words flow through my soul. I plan to accomplish this, but for now that thought is gently stored in a deep crevice of my mind, sure to emerge at another time.

Continual curiosity leads me to wonder if there are others like me who spontaneously speak languages they haven't studied. If so, is anyone currently doing research on such a phenomenon? Could this phenomenon be common and I just wasn't aware of it? Little did I know that this inquisitive fork in the road was about to define my future.

Turning to the Internet once again I searched with a dual purpose. I needed to discover the whys and hows of this language. I was satisfied that the channeled languages coming through were valid and of importance, but I wanted to learn more. Searching seemed interminable while I sought answers to the unexplainable. Couldn't I just access the Akashic Records and find *The Book of Janet's Life,* and page to the right chapter for a quick explanation? If only life were that simple. Instead I was counting on diligence, faith, and luck.

Feeling guided by an unseen hand, I found myself at the website of Dr. Charles Tart, Ph.D. His research encompassed a wide range of thought-provoking subjects from altered states to mindful living. I sent him an email, explaining my situation and what I was searching for. He emailed back that although my story was fascinating, it fell outside of his expertise, but he offered to pass my email along to some of his colleagues, to which I readily agreed. Ready and waiting, I hoped someone would email me back, and soon.

Within days I received a number of emails. Some were interested in my story from a general stand point. One man told me he was very interested, however he was busy working on an experiment at the time and could I email him back in five months when his project would be complete. His name was Dr. Gary Schwartz, Ph.D. Waiting five months was nothing compared to the four years I had previously waited until I found Ipu. Then when he mentioned experiments I had to wonder, what kind? I was intrigued. Maybe he would be interested in testing my languages? It sounded interesting—then again, I was actually hoping for answers, not really looking for an experiment. I emailed him back that I would send him a message in five months.

Time flew by and I emailed him again in August. To my surprise he responded immediately only to say he was still in the middle of something, but he encouraged me to check back in five or six months. Disappointed, but not discouraged, I chose to have patience and try one last time in six months.

February 6, 2001, arrived and I shot off a last-chance email. If he wasn't interested this time, I was going to move on. Someone heard my plea, because I received a phone number and a time to call when he would be available.

My first impression of Dr. Schwartz was that of a very busy professor. He showed interest in my language phenomenon, but mentioned he was currently involved in a number of other projects. When I asked what they were about, he suggested I read his book, that it would explain his work in more detail. The book is *The Living Energy Universe*, coauthored by Linda Russek Ph.D. As I hung up the phone I decided he was sincere in his interest to help me, but perhaps too busy to do so. It looked like more Internet searching lay ahead of me. In the meantime, finding the book title and the man fascinating, I purchased the book.

It was March 21, 2001, when I emailed Dr. Schwartz for the last time. I shared my thoughts. The email simply stated that I enjoyed the personal stories mixed in with the professional viewpoints. Email sent, it was time to move forward and find someone else that had time and would be willing to help me now.

Two days later, after sending the email something amazing, even extraordinary, transpired.

On March 23, 2001, I was relaxing in a chair when a woman I've never met appeared to me out of thin air. A strong vision projected through my mind as if she was standing in my great room and I hear, "Susy, Susy, Susy." The words rhythmically pulsed through my thoughts like a mantra— "Susy, Susy, Susy." This woman almost felt familiar, but I couldn't place her. She looked opaque and was standing behind a leather wingback chair in my great room. She looked thin, had whitish hair, she was wearing a dress that seemed light in color, however, standing behind and to the side a bit, I couldn't be sure of the color because her dress had a glowing effect to it. She stared fixedly at me. Drawn to her face, I heard in my mind, "I am with Sam." I glanced around the room but couldn't see anyone else. She quickly grabbed her chest as if to show she was having a heart attack. Like watching a live game of charades, I could sense the feeling and I began to panic. Suddenly, as if struck by lightning, I knew who this woman was. The air was close and all of my attention was directed at this woman. This was Susy Smith, not just any Susy, but the one from Gary's book. Oh my gosh, this woman had died. With that, the vision faded back into the shadows from which it came.

Utterly shocked by this connection, I let out a breath I had been holding for what seemed like an eternity. Jumping up and running to the office, I immediately sent emails to both Gary and Linda. I shared with them what Susy showed me visually. I was amazed that this woman who I never knew came through to me, and wondered why. After sending the emails, I sat contemplating this surprising occurrence—I wasn't afraid.

And with that twist of fate, a new journey began to unfold...

Chapter Eight
A Push from the Other Side

I said to myself, I have things in my head that are not like what anyone has taught me - shapes and ideas so near to me - so natural to my way of being and thinking that it hasn't occurred to me to put them down. I decided to start anew, to strip away what I had been taught.
Georgia O'Keeffe

Dr. Schwartz received my email about Susy and immediately shot one back. He verified that Susy had indeed died, and only a month before. Learning of Susy's recent death lead me to believe she wasn't wasting any time on the other side. He also stated she had died from a heart attack. This unexpected validation pushed him to ask me for more: "Could Susy come through again?" Against my own common sense, I reluctantly agreed to try. After all, I didn't know this man, I was having difficulty pinning him down, and suddenly he wants something from me I wasn't sure I could provide. However, I decided a little effort couldn't hurt. Seeking out Susy the following morning, while sitting at the computer, I asked out loud as I stared at the blank celadon wall before me, "Ok Susy, if you're around, can you show me another vision?"

She was around alright. My relationship with Susy via visions soon became one of student to mentor and I came to look upon our connection as a gift bestowed upon me. She became a blessing in disguise. Susy came through in my daily meditation and literally blasted through my fears from the past. For some reason I trusted this mature woman. She showed me visions of daily life, but often these were confusing and I would email Dr. Schwartz a jumble of what seemed to be useless information. Susy often sent me the same vision again and again, until I could understand them. There were many lessons for me to learn, often difficult ones. Unfortunately, I wasn't the best student, and to make matters worse, this was a "course" I had only reluctantly signed up for. I would begin by typing something she revealed to me, then a feeling of doubt would overcome me as I realized I had used the wrong words to describe her vision. Frustrated that her vision wasn't black and white to me, I had to start over with a new description that varied substantially from the first attempt. If I was confident when finished, I would send it to Dr. Schwartz, otherwise I'd sit there staring at the screen, wondering if I was psychotic. *What led me to this point in my life again?* It was often surreal. An important lesson to learn was to take myself out of the way, not to assume or interpret. Not to describe what I *thought* I saw, but what was actually being shown in a vision before my eyes—there often was a big difference. It must have been a chore for Susy to work within *my own frame of reference from my personal life experiences* and *how I personally relate to things emotionally.* There were times when she showed me something so off the wall that I would sit and laugh out loud, trying to relate her message as exact as possible, because I couldn't possibly come up with something so bizarre on my own! Dr. Schwartz emailed me vague comments on how the visions pertained to something he was involved in, but basically kept me in the dark. He even mentioned at times that he couldn't discuss the situation for scientific reasons. I wondered what in the heck was he talking about.

After a number of weeks, Dr. Schwartz asked if I wanted to continue this email dialogue with visions from Susy. I thought it was a fantastic idea as long as Susy continued to appear. We could see what would manifest. Since he knew Susy and I didn't, I needed his expertise to confirm or deny what I was being shown. Susy graced me with small insights into her own life, one I knew nothing about. It was left up to Dr. Schwartz to decide if what I received was accurate or not. When we decided to continue this email dialogue, Dr. Schwartz suggested I call him Gary.

Unbeknownst to me, Gary had begun his first "informal experiment." My morning routine now included an email to Gary with anything Susy chose to show me. This all seemed like it was emerging from a science fiction novel, only it was real. It was my day-to-day life. Sometimes, very straightforward information would emerge. Susy was taking her time with me, showing a sense of humor in one email, a warning in another.

I emailed Gary:

Susy shows me your car, I can see a light through your steering wheel on the dashboard, and it's flashing.

Sure enough Gary wrote back:

That's true, I need an oil change and the light comes on when I start the car, flashing a reminder.

Once Susy showed herself dancing, enjoying herself immensely. I didn't know what this meant, but somehow it seemed important, so I sent it to Gary. Later I learned she had been confined to a wheelchair toward the end of her life, so I think she was trying to show us that she was now free of the human body and living it up.

Many months later, I was told Susy had communicated with other mediums and she also showed one of them that she was dancing. It helped validate my own vision and the process from two separate mediums who had never met or even knew each other at the time. This is a perfect example of how Gary kept me in the dark months at a time for the sake of research.

I often received visions from Susy about accidents. The visions were nothing like those I'd seen as a young adult. This time around, emotion was somehow removed, as if watching a movie, instead of acting in it. It's possible that typing out the visions as they emerged didn't give me the chance to experience the emotion, because I was always waiting for the next scene to appear. Maybe typing words on paper dilutes the emotion to some extent. This led me to realize my meditative state didn't stop when I began typing. I was in a kind of visual trance like state of meditation as my fingers pounded away at the keyboard. Receiving information simultaneously from Susy while typing was quite an awakening. I never realized it was possible for me to do this. Maybe this is how the term "inspirational writing" was coined. It would make sense that we receive inspiration from the other side or from our higher selves. So why not receive it from loved ones and friends who are over there to help us progress in our human journey? So much to wonder about!

Aware something important was taking place, I've kept every email. I also wanted proof for myself, as well as for others, because I was convinced no one would possibly believe this. Hell, I had a hard time believing it. Yet every day I woke up anticipating what visions Susy would show me, then wait to see how Gary would reply. What a trip!

In the beginning it was difficult for me to ask Susy a question and then wait for a reply, because it was hard to maintain my focus. I gradually became better, but in the end, I realized she was going to give me what she wanted and that was that. I had to believe she knew what was best for me at the time. If we got our answer, great—if not, Gary and I dealt with it.

The encounters with Susy turned my visions into a learning experience and made me crave to be a clearer channel. Instead of fighting and fearing it for so many years, I now wanted to see everything that was possibly attainable. My fear was diminished by crossing paths with this treasure of a woman named Susy. She replaced my childhood fears with a new world of discovery and exploration. Age and experience may have played a small role as well. No longer did I wander in the fearful tangled labyrinths of life, instead I was venturing out to see the other side. I now knew I was meant to share this ability. Each time I tried to push it aside, it muscled its way back in again and again, manifesting in its own unique way. I am thankful and honored for the many lessons Susy has taught me.

***

I would like to share some of the three hundred emails that I sent to Gary about Susy's visions, along with his responses. Many contain personal information specifically relating to Gary or someone around him, so those will stay private. In other cases, Gary chose not to answer for experimental purposes. I truly begun to believe that his favorite line was, "I need to keep you in the dark." This often led to replies that made little or no sense.

After reading Gary's responses, you'll have an understanding of exactly what I'm talking about, as well as how I remained constantly perplexed.

Hi Gary,
   Susy is showing me that she is swimming.
   She also shows CA, AZ and NY........Shows you're traveling to them soon.

Gary replies:
   Hi----Susy loved to swim and you showing her swimming is very meaningful to me, as well as for other reasons.

Also NY, CA, and AZ are very significant at this time. I will be traveling to all of them.

* * *

OK Gary,

Today Susy is really pushy. Kind of pushy in a sweet, yet tough older lady kind of way...........Anyway I have to ask, do you have Susy's heart in a jar to study? I know that sounds bizarre, but that is what she is showing me.

Gary replies:

Hi----No, Susy agreed to have her heart in a jar to study, but there were complications and the medical school could not follow through with Susy's plan.

* * *

Hi Gary,

..........I heard Susy say "crap" and it came out loud!........I can't believe I'm telling you this.....

Gary replies: Susy would say "crap," she was VERY DIRECT........with her thoughts.

* * *

Hi Gary,

.....Susy shows me people surfing of all things! Don't know how that relates to you! I also hear a song: "Send in the Clowns!" She is jumping from one thing to the next very fast today........Well, hope you have a great day.....Mine started out a little crazy here!

Gary replies:

"Send in the Clowns" is one of my favorite songs! I will be at a place soon where people surf.

***

105

Hi Gary,

Today begins with Susy showing me "Hot Air Balloons" and bright colors of the rainbows. Yes, a rainbow is what I'm seeing.

Next I am seeing the word "crane" …..Oh wait, it's a bird. And for some reason I am connecting this to an Indian ceremony or something like that around you. Kind of unusual if you ask me…then again….

Now I hear Susy telling me you are going "back"….and I feel I'm taken back to my childhood.

Gary replies:

You were virtually 98% accurate below. I was in Indian country and purchased some key Indian art as a memento. Rainbows were very important this weekend, must run…

At one point, Gary decided to ask a direct question to Susy and have her tell me in some way what he asked. I was up for this little experimental challenge and hoped it would come through clearly. Weeks drifted by, Susy supposedly showed me everything "around it," but I never saw the exact thing Gary was asking Susy for. It was frustrating, yet it also made me realize we can't always get the "exact" thing someone is wanting, for confirmation. For whatever reason in this case it didn't manifest. Susy could show a picture to me in details, such as the color of the picture frame and the people in it. She showed me a picture window, a fountain through that window, but never the exact thing that Gary asked. Needless to say Gary never did tell me what it was he was asking. Once again, I was left in the dark.

Gary often questioned how my psychic and medium ability worked. Some days, I received an abundance of information, other days not so much. There were times when I would smell something, other times see a vision and even on occasion hear words or sounds. Gary was currently working with other mediums and understood you can't fit all mediums into one mold. If Medium "X" can see visions, but Medium "Y" can't, why is that? Human experiences are molded by thought processes and life itself. I believe the same is true for mediums' abilities. Experiencing that first vision or sixth-sense drives our future and allows us to be open to more of the same. Which direction we expand is up to us. It's the same for anyone. If you give a painter a crayon he can still create art with it, but since crayons are not his preferred medium he may not do as well as if he had his brushes. Every medium has their own way of accessing their abilities. Luckily, Gary understands that we all have our own quirks in the way we work, which make us the unique mediums we are.

Below, I would like to show how, at times, Gary would answer an email and keep me in the dark simultaneously, satisfying me that I did receive something pertinent.

Gold coins…two people understand this that I forwarded the email to.
Watering hole…
horse……
Gary replies: Yes, it relates….

"And then that would be it?"…………I would think to myself……."you're kidding, that's it?" There is no way I could know what was going on in his life. I can't understand it myself. But then he would say: "It relates, keep it up!"
And so, I did.

* * *

Hi Gary,
Yesterday Susy came through with something about Romans and the Coliseum?
What's that about?
Gary replies: I was just reading about Rome and the Roman Empire…………

* * *

Hi Gary,
Susy is showing a greenhouse, then she jumps to circles or something circular in shape. Next I get a flash of a medicine wheel…wait, now Susy is showing me a telescope and I look through it to see the stars, although not the *placement it seems* of certain stars. Last I see her showing me an astrology chart or what looks like one. Hm…..
Gary replies: this is AMAZING…..I've been reading about the Secret Life of Plants and we looked into conducting research at greenhouses. Also reading True Esoteric Traditions, which relates to this. I went to a conference and it was all about telescopes, looking into the sky seeing patterns from the micro to the macro…….and medicine wheels, all part of the picture.

***

Hi Gary,

Woke up this morning with a couple things that popped into my head. It didn't feel like it came from Susy but maybe so.

First, I see a plane crash with people who are dark complexioned.........
and last I saw the two tallest buildings in the world, The Twin Petronas Towers. Something on the lower left side, an explosion? A fire? I pray it doesn't happen.

Gary replied: Keep this email.

Months later I realized it wasn't the Twin Petronas Towers, also known as the Twin Towers, but the World Trade Center towers....

I feel this email was extremely significant. It showed a precognitive event, on a scale I never imagined possible. How I knew and felt it beforehand still blows me away to this day. One simple email, separate from Susy's visions, reminded me, we're all so much more than human. It also made me realize that, no matter what I get or not, no matter how I wish to change something, it may still happen. We can't prevent, stop or change everything. I wish we could, but that's not possible.

A couple of months before that fateful morning of 9-11, I went to bed each night in a routine manner. Within an hour of falling asleep, I would suddenly jolt up into a sitting position and grab at my throat. Eerie sounds of distress forced their way from my lungs and vocal cords as if gasping for air. Minutes would tick by until my breathing and pounding heart returned to a more normal pace. I would then lie down and try to get back to sleep. This happened almost on a nightly basis. Many nights I would scare the hell out of my husband. Startled awake, he would wonder what was going on, as I was grasping my throat and sometimes crying. Carl and I both thought it was extremely odd for that to just suddenly begin to happen. We came to the conclusion I was possibly having some sort of sleep disorder, so I contacted a sleep lab. I set up an appointment for the third week of September. The sleep lab had just opened a couple of months before, they were heavily booked and this was the earliest I could get in. They told me that if I felt my problem was getting too bad or if it got worse at any time to head to the emergency room immediately. I couldn't explain it, but I knew something was off. This didn't make sense for my sleep to be interrupted to such a dramatic extent. Yet, every night I would wake up, propelling myself upright with this constant shaking and grabbing at my throat. I tried to explain to Carl that the source felt outside of me. It was almost as if someone were trying to tell me something, but I just couldn't figure it out. Until the morning of 9-11-01. That changed everything.

Mourning with the rest of America, thoughts of 9-11 were constantly on my mind. It wasn't until days later, I realized I wasn't having any more unusual sleeping problems. Whereas many now had difficulty sleeping, I was back to a somewhat regular sleeping pattern, minus the times I awoke to relive the horror many of us saw on the news or in person. I truly believe I was picking up on the energy of this horrible event that was already being set into place. I guess being empathic, it didn't matter if I was asleep or awake, it was still coming through. On some level, I already understood that it was out there. Once the event took place, that energy had changed by some force I couldn't begin to explain. I canceled my appointment at the sleep lab and I've never had it happen since.

* * *

Gary and I both experienced times when we would try to send an email to each other and the computer would do something crazy, like shut down on its own, have strange colors flash across the screen, and lose emails in the midst of typing them. At times when I would lose an email in cyberspace, I took it as a sign that I wasn't getting the correct information. I assumed that it was just Susy making me retype it. She could be one hell of an energy force.

As time moved on, I continued emailing Gary, Monday through Friday. I was diligent about my morning meditation emails with Susy, although I did take the weekends off. So I had an unexpected shock one delightful Saturday morning in October. A week after purchasing my new white car something utterly amazing happened. So astounding, I almost crashed Casper, the name of my car I humorously dubbed.

The dealership where we bought my car was a half-hour away from my home and I needed to drop some papers off to them. It was a relaxing drive on a beautiful autumn day, with a fall palette of trees in oranges, reds and gold. Passing by the rolling hills, driving with the windows down and enjoying the wind blowing through my hair I sped along to the tunes on the stereo. Out of nowhere, Susy pops in. As I veered toward the median, I quickly corrected to avoid it. Heart pounding, I almost crashed my brand new car.

Apparently, I'm not the calm Psychic Medium I thought I was. In the back of my mind I thought, *"Damn it Susy, you scared the shit out of me."* Susy didn't seem to notice as she went on to deliver information, as if we did this every day of the week, only this time she had a woman with her, and I was driving.

There is a time and a place for everything, and driving along the highway just over the speed limit is not a good time for a lot of things. I pulled over to the shoulder, opened the glove box and jotted down the quick visions I was given on the back of an envelope. Astonished over this unforeseen event, I then got back on the highway and drove home. I wasn't really sure at first if I should email Gary or wait until Monday. However, Susy's surprise visit was extremely unusual and influenced my immediate decision. I thought what-the-heck, and sent the email off to him. After sending it, I started thinking I needed to have a little chat with Susy because I really did not want to meet her up close and personal anytime soon. Besides, I had just bought Casper and I was planning on keeping him for a long time.

I received an email from Gary on Monday morning in reply to my Saturday email. He explained he had been with a woman and her family over the weekend. He noticed how much pain this woman was in over the loss of her sister. He thought to himself how blessed he felt that Susy was still coming through, via myself and other mediums, and how he wished this woman's sister would come through for her. Here's the clincher: He was thinking this while in the car with them.

Screech........back it up......did he just say that in his email? He explained that he had received my email on Saturday in New York, when I never in the past had emailed him, and that he had called the woman on Sunday afternoon. He read her what I sent and asked her to informally score the reading, which turned out to be more than 80% accurate.

This gave Gary the idea for the Double-Deceased Paradigm.........What Susy did was bring the unknown (deceased) sister to Gary, through me. Susy had just invented a new experiment from the other side, the double-blind experiment, with the help of Gary and myself.

It became an important moment in the history of his mediumship research. Gary discovered a new way to try a more difficult experiment for testing mediums. Did Susy and I just work overtime? Maybe it was a reminder to continue carrying lots of car insurance in the future? Joking aside, this situation implied much more than I could ever have imagined.

I got a message across to a family I had never met, and who resided in

New York. Their sister, who loved them from beyond life, sent comforting information to them through Susy and myself. The timing was impeccable. This in turn helped create a new experiment that taught others to see that loved ones often come through in many ways, through many people, even to those they don't know, simply out of love. An incredible lesson was learned that day. One should never assume a message can come through only in one way or even through only one person. Susy showed us, it can emerge in whatever way it needs to.

One personal request I stated loudly to Susy was, "From now on, step away from the car!" I also told Gary, "Next time, wait until you're out of a moving vehicle to ask Susy something!"

He laughed.

It was during moments like this I had no self-doubt about what I was supposed to be doing in life. Since then, Gary has fine-tuned and tested this double-blind experiment multiple times with a number of mediums, including myself, before he conducted formal experiments. This was an interesting experiment since you never had any opportunity to speak with the person you were reading, called "the sitter." A proxy, research assistant, or experimenter was your only connection. They met the person that was to be read, but the medium never did. This methodology was used to rule out cold readings, visual and auditory cues and fraud. After each reading was complete, it would be scored. The fascinating extra to this experiment was the fact that not only did the sitter not hear the reading as it was happening, but when they went to score it they were given two readings to review. One was theirs and the other was for a different sitter. They were being tested to learn if they had received enough information to show validity with their deceased loved one or not. Gary later created the triple-blind experiments. Not only did the medium continue to be blind to who was being read, but a proxy, research assistant or experimenter was used who had no prior knowledge about the sitter either. They were only given a first name for the sitter, so that no one could accuse the medium of reading the experimenter's mind by the use of telepathy. I was thrilled to be a part of the process in connection with the experiments that were being created. Considering Gary was a scientist whose motto is, "Let the data speak," I realized that when the data did speak, you had better pay attention.

Chapter Nine

Discoveries

*When people keep telling you that you can't do
a thing, you kind of like to try it.*
Margaret Chase Smith

Being tested formally and informally at the Human Energy Systems Laboratory (HESL) was a continuous learning experience—exploring the depth of my abilities was empowering. I was always willing to be challenged by Dr. Schwartz and whatever new experiment he and his collaborator Julie Beischel, Ph.D. could create. One of the formal experiments that I participated in can be found in Dianne Arcangel's book; *Afterlife Encounters.* There you will learn about the process and procedures implemented during a formal reading. Although honored and grateful for the opportunity to be tested, it was often the unforeseen events that would occur during or after an experiment that added more depth to a reading. I believe the combination brought even more validation. Below are a couple of instances to give you an idea of how such events manifested.

Accident Waiting to Happen

One case happened in July of 2002, when a formal email experiment with the HESL was in progress. This experimental study began Monday and would run each morning until Friday. Five different people referred to as research "sitters" were used in this study. My job was to email the research assistant, in this case Chris Baker, what I received each morning from Spirit. I asked Susy to be my spirit guide in this experiment, knowing our connection was a good one. I had absolutely no idea who these people were, and was given no information except an email with the first name only, the evening before the formal experiment. During this time there would be no contact or emails with Dr. Schwartz. My only connection to the research aspect was Chris. Once the visions were received from Susy, I emailed them to the research assistant and the experiment was then considered complete for that day. We were finished until the experiment began again the next morning—a pretty cut-and-dry experiment, or so it seemed.

It wasn't until later that week, while reporting what I was receiving from Susy, that my TV turned itself off. Okay, now you're probably asking yourself, "Why does she even have a TV on while doing a formal experiment?" It's simply a habit, I like the positive vibration I feel from it even though I have the volume on mute and I'm not watching it. Besides myself, there was no one else in the house when this happened. Getting up, grabbing the remote, I hit the power button and it came on without a hitch. It made me stop and take note. Could this be some kind of warning or Susy telling me to turn it off? I had no idea. I do know the other side has been known to manipulate electronics, so I simply took note and thanked whoever was stopping by and continued with my meditation.

Satisfied with the morning experiment, it was time to get moving—it never seemed like there were enough hours in the day to get everything completed and my day was packed full. While running errands, a sudden, intense vision flashed before my eyes which left me paralyzed on the spot. Luckily, I was sitting at a stop sign and not driving. I saw an image of someone walking up to a grocery store, then a car came barreling out of nowhere and almost hit them. The vision jerked me back into reality, shivers running down my spine. I had this immediate impression that this vision was for one of the sitters in the five-day experiment I was currently participating in. The need to relay the information immediately propelled me to drive home without delay. Pulling in the garage, running through the house and into the office, I sat down in a rush. Quickly shooting off an email to the research assistant, I explained the vision that prompted me to contact him. I asked Chris if he could please send my message out to the sitters as a warning. Since I had no idea who these people were, it was going to be left up to Chris to get the job done.

Later that evening I received an email back from Chris. He stated that within an hour after he sent the email, a response came in saying that one of the sitters almost got hit by a car while walking into the store. He also mentioned the sitter was pretty shook up. Although I didn't know who the message was for, I did know where to send it. And it was obvious, a connection was made. Two thumbs up for Susy.

***

Casper

This story is presented to demonstrate how loved ones are often nearby and watching over us. Something extreme doesn't need to happen for them to drop in. It could simply be for support in any area of our lives. Sometimes they appear to acknowledge things that are happening and remind us that they see it as well. Just because they left their body, doesn't mean they aren't around in Spirit.

This spontaneous reading happened months after conducting a formal experiment at the HESL. It was for a sitter, whom I didn't know nor had ever met. The only connection was a first name given during the formal experiment.

The alarm clock penetrated my sleep-fogged mind and as I leaned over to turn it off, it was then I felt a presence near the bed. Eyes popping open, glancing around, the room appeared empty. Confident it was someone coming through from the other side made me hurry out of bed and scurry through my morning routine. As my son left for school, the door closing behind him, the house settled into stillness. It was then I heard the name Casper as if manifesting out of thin air. I immediately knew who was dropping by for a visit. This specific Spirit, whom I dubbed Casper during a formal reading with HESL, was popping in for some curious reason. The problem arose over the fact I couldn't just email his parents, because I didn't know who they were. I had to go through the HESL to speak with his family because our connection was through the lab. Walking into my office, I sat down and began typing the messages that were flowing through. Pounding rhythmically at the keys, the email started to take shape.

Casper, as I warmly called him, is actually John Kaspari. This young

115

man lost his life in a motorcycle accident. For him to drop in many months after a reading made me believe he had something important to share.

First, he began with a birthday or congratulations and some sort of celebration around this time of year. He wanted to acknowledge something of importance that was happening at this time and it was directed towards his family. John next showed me something having to do with his eyes and it felt like it related to his father.

He then went on to share that someone recently joined him on the other side because he was making me feel like there is someone "new" over there. With that, I had a feeling of an image of someone eating noodles or pasta. I assumed this person was a big pasta eater.

And finally a question formed in my mind: *Did John's father recently bump his head? It feels like this happened on the right front side.* Interestingly, I felt a pressure on my right front forehead when this thought came though. Needing to warn him if this hadn't already happened, I hoped to give him a heads up (no pun intended). Added to that, I stated at the bottom of the email that it felt as if something important needed to be acknowledged, possibly a special date he wanted his father to take note of. In closing I stated that John seems happy and his energy continues to feel like he's a free spirit. I actually heard the song playing in my mind, "Born to Be Wild."

I sent the email to Dr. Julie Beischel, the principal research investigator at the lab, and asked her to please forward it to John's father.

It was shortly thereafter, that I received a direct reply from John's dad, Bill. He first offered a thanks for the brief reading. Bill stated that at first as he began reading the email, it didn't seem to be anything of significance, until he got to the part about, "Did John's father recently bump his head on the right front side?"

Bill's reply was that no, he hadn't bumped his head, however when he went to his daughter's house, she had her husband show him a huge bump, black eye and cut over his right eye. The night before, he had walked into the corner of a wall in their house. Bill stated he found this more than a small coincidence, especially since it just happened.

Bill then spoke to his wife, Diane, about the comment related to a birthday or celebration. Once again, not directly in the family, but of interest was the fact that his wife was supposed to attend a baby shower that day for a good friend's son and daughter-in-law. She received a phone call early that same morning that the expectant mom was in the hospital in labor and the shower was canceled. John was friends with the new dad.

Bill next wrote of the person who had recently passed. It related to a woman that Diane knew and therefore I won't go into too much detail. Suffice to say, Diane asked a woman who she knew had died, to please help the family cope with her loss. She felt that this was the woman's way of letting her know (from John, to me) that she heard her and believes this could be the main reason for the email. And last, the pasta connection: Bill explained that Diane commented on a conversation she had with John the night before he passed. He told her he was having macaroni and cheese for dinner. Just one more small synchronicity. Bill thanked me for the reading and was happy to know John was still around.

It was shortly after that I received a second email from Bill asking questions about the reading itself. I thought this would be the perfect opportunity to share my answers to his insightful questions about how I received information.

Bill questioned:
1. When you said, "Also did John's father recently bump his head on the right front side?" can you describe the image, if there was an image that led you to make this comment? If it was an image, was it one you have of my son John or some other person? I am curious to know if it might fit my son-in-law who actually hit his head the night before or if it was perhaps John showing you something using his image.

2. You made comments about "a birthday or congrats but I am seeing a celebration coming from him" and "I also feel like someone recently joined him that he knows because he is making me feel like someone new is with him."
Can you describe the way in which you sensed these messages? Were they images, just feelings, a combination of the two or something else?

I replied:

Hi Bill,
I'll try to answer your questions as best I can.
First, let me explain that from what I can recall of that morning, I

believe shortly after I woke up I felt someone was around me. So, I already knew I was about to find out something from someone on the other side. After my son left for school and I began the day I suddenly heard the name "Casper" and stopped short. That triggered an immediate Spirit person for me since John Kaspari is the only person I relate to with that name. So I asked: "Is this John?" As I walked into the office I decided to just sit down and type whatever came through right away so I wouldn't lose the connection.

I couldn't see John, but I felt his presence. Having this ability gave me the awareness that someone wanted to come through. The next thought was triggered by the word "Casper" that I heard. Not beside my ear, but inside my head, like those times when a word comes into your thoughts and you can't let go of it.

Before I move on, let me explain. I hear Spirit voices at times as if they speak directly in my ear, but usually I hear a name or word in my mind. Does that make sense? Unfortunately I don't hear whole sentences or paragraphs, just a word here and there. A perfect example of this would be when you're on the cell phone and it cuts out. You may hear: Bill…. cleaners…Chinese…home. So I would take that as: Hi Bill, I'm running to the cleaners, then I'll grab some Chinese food and head home. It's the same sort of concept for me. I assemble the puzzle pieces to create the message. I try not to interpret, but at times I'm at a loss for how else to convey a message. So, I do the best I can and try to keep it as close as possible to the way I hear it.

Let's say John feels the "need" to get a message across for whatever reason. He is only given a small amount of time, so he has to give me what he can in as few visions, thoughts, or words as possible. It may be just the way I personally work, that I can only hold the energy for a given amount of time. For whatever reason, it works in that way, and it's possible John knows that as well. I won't even try to imagine the how or why of that statement.

So he came to me because:

*I was open that day?

*I had a connection to him in the past reading through an experiment?

*He knows I'll try to get the message across to you, through the lab via Dr. Beischel?

It could be any reason, I'm just the vessel into which it came.

Dr. Schwartz and Dr. Beischel could explain that I often get "drop-ins" and friends from past readings, as if my connections with them still hold. So, why did he come to me and not you? Maybe he did come to you, but you weren't really "sure" at the time or you weren't paying attention. Perhaps he comes through to someone he knows will hear him. Or in a way that will give an impact to his short statements so you do pay attention.

Now to the reading.

1. Can you describe the image when you said, "Also did John's father recently bump his head on the right front side?"—if there was an image that led you to make this comment. If it was an image, was it one you have of my son John or some other person? I am curious to know if it might fit my son-in-law who actually hit his head the night before, or if it was perhaps John showing you something using his image.

Okay, once I figured out it was John he gave me some information. I actually felt like I bumped my head and I felt it on the right front side. I knew John was trying to "impress an energy" to me that someone bumped their head. I thought it was for you, Bill, because I asked Dr. Beischel to send you the email. It felt male. Since I had you and the bump and a male feeling, I said you. This is where I also learn from a reading. I'm sure Dr. Schwartz is shaking his head about now. He would ask why didn't I just say a male connected to Bill? Well, perhaps because in this case I made an assumption, which is something I know I shouldn't do. Male...Bill... bump on his head...the right side. Sounds logical at least. Bill bumped his head on the right side. So I need to work on that area, at least it helps me for next time. I always work towards getting it exactly right, and in this case I was close. It was a bump on the right side and it was related to you, Bill, even if it wasn't you. However, the message did get across and was received and verified—so it did in fact work. As for the scientific side, it's a work in progress.

2. You made comments about "a birthday or congrats but I am seeing a celebration coming from him," and "I also feel like someone recently joined him that he knows because he is making me feel like someone "new" is with him."

Can you describe the way in which you sensed these messages? Were they images, just feelings, a combination of the two or something else?

119

Okay, these questions are a little easier, but tricky as well. I've already established that I knew John came through. So when I see a young man holding a cake with a candle, I know it's a celebration related to him and not something from my own unique symbolism. I saw that as an actual vision. Energy coming through appeared positive and I felt his warm smile. So this message was definitely a happy occasion. John was essentially showing me props and at the same time making me feel good. So I had two simultaneous impressions of the circumstance, visions and feelings. Now I couldn't tell you what he looked like exactly, but I did have a hair impression at the time. Nice hair or hair I would like, kind of wild or a little longer. No clue why I would get that. I also saw a zipper, so that led me to believe he had a jacket on. To me the quick little messages that he was sending held importance so I better make note of it. It's the least I can do.

Now the cake disappears quickly and he then shows me a new, relatively short, person standing next to him. I can't say I clearly saw the person, but I knew and felt that they had recently passed. Now, how do I know this? By the "energy" I was feeling. It wasn't a person who's been there for a while. I guess you could compare it to a new employee. It often takes a while for them to fit in the groove and get adjusted to a new place. He wanted me to let you know he's aware of what's going on. It's that simple and that complicated. Hopefully these explanations are helpful to you. You could look at it as if John has given each of you—your daughter, your wife and yourself—a little piece of himself. John said a lot in such a short, impromptu reading.

Thanks again for caring enough to send your messages.
No problem!

This short ten-minute email reading shows you just one of the many ways in which our loved ones are willing to come through to get a message across to us. They really are with you at times. John didn't mind sending me the message which then had to go through the lab, and then on to his dad. As long as he got the message across, that's all that matters. Pay attention, listen and be open the next time you think a message from a loved one comes through in a way you believed was not possible. Stop and ask yourself, "Why not?" Accept it with grace, gratitude and at face value and you won't go wrong.

Bailey

Every reading is individual, personal and unique to the person I am reading.

Bailey first came through during a formal lab experiment—a new experiment was being implemented, which brought on new challenges and a new format. In addition to the reading we normally did, a new section called the "Asking Question Study" was added. In this section of the experiment, the principal research investigator, Dr. Beischel, would ask fifty questions about the deceased while their loved one, whom was never mentioned, would listen on a phone line with no voice activation. During this experiment, as in all the experiments, no feedback was given to the medium throughout the entire reading. It wasn't until over a year later that I found out my results, and who was listening on the other phone line. Formal lab experiments require extreme amounts of time and patience for everyone involved. Not only does the reading have to be transcribed, but the sitter then has to score the reading for accuracy. When I received the results of Bailey's reading over a year later, I was honored to learn the reading carried substantial validation for her parents, Phran who was the sitter, her husband Bob, her brother Jon, and sister Kori.

Months later, it was early morning and I was driving my son and the car pool kids to school. A van full of sleepy kids mumbling stories about the previous day and last night's homework filled the air. As I turned into the school parking lot, I followed the line of cars to the drop-off area. As the kids piled out of the van I suddenly felt this somewhat familiar spirit presence, and it was Bailey. Imagine being in the school parking lot and this teenage girl I've met only in spirit form, and read once during a lab experiment, drops in and is sitting next to me in the passenger seat. Talk about surprises! I suddenly have this vision running free rein in my mind while I'm surrounded by cars filled with children being dropped off for school. All I can think about is leaving the parking lot and getting home because I have a message to deliver! First things first: leave the lot safely, pull out onto the main street and then cut through the subdivision and get home. Although the vision lasted less than 30 seconds, I knew that for whatever reason she came through I had to make sure I got her message across. Here we go again….

I pulled in the driveway, jumped out and ran inside. I sat down at the computer and began pounding away at the keys. I emailed Dr. Beischel at the lab. I explained what happened and asked if she could please send my email to Bailey's mom. As usual she was happy to forward any messages.

Hours later I received an email back from Bailey's mom, Phran. She wanted to verify the information I sent her from Bailey. You see, Bailey came in to show me her mom was working at the breakfast room table, surrounded by big windows around her. Bailey showed me she had candles lit as well. She was showing me what her mom was doing at the exact time the vision came. She wanted to just let her know she could see her and that she was with her. Since the only thing I knew about Bailey and her family was what Bailey showed me through visions during a formal experimental reading with HESL, I had no clue whether a breakfast room or big windows existed or if candles were lit in her honor.

Phran informed me she lit candles for Bailey every morning. To me, it was this activity Bailey wanted me to relay. Phran also mentioned that working in the breakfast room at that hour was out of the ordinary, since she normally was in her office by then. It was after this email that Phran and I began talking and soon became friends. I credit Bailey with this gifted connection.

I was blessed to have this new found friendship with Bailey's parents, Phran and Bob. Bailey's energy is a ray of sunshine that has touched many. For her to reach out to me is one of the loveliest gifts I could have received. Just those few special moments make my past struggles worth every fear I've encountered.

I had the opportunity to ask Phran and Bob if they had any expectations going into the reading. They shared that they had a number of private readings already, a very expensive group reading and even a séance, so by now they were open-minded and receptive to whatever might or might not come through. However, it was clear that they wanted to connect to Bailey more than anything else in the entire world. Phran informed me she was the sitter on the other end of the phone the day the reading occurred and further added, "In the many opportunities I have had to connect with Bailey and the other side, both before and after my reading with you, Janet, there were only two cases when the information was so abundant and accurate that it left no doubt about the existence of a non-physical world. Your sitting was one of them. I cannot therefore single out any one or two, or even three things that may have stood out. The information is all just too significant for that. In addition, it is now more than 19 months later, and rereading my notes from the sitting seems even more powerful in ascertaining the survival of consciousness and, more so, the evidence that Bailey has not left the room!"

Phran and Bob Ginsberg have since created Forever Family Foundation to further the understanding of afterlife science through research and education while providing support and healing for people in grief. You can learn more about Forever Family Foundation at www. ForeverFamilyFoundation.org

***

As I continued working with Dr. Schwartz and Dr. Beischel on research experiments, I also provided private readings. I would like to share some validating stories, events and connections that emerged during a handful of readings. Some names and places have been altered for reasons of privacy.

***

The Car

I repeated to the three individuals sitting before me, "Tony keeps showing me a car with the hood up." Tony's mom, sister and brother-in-law sat quietly as I continued, "A wire or battery charger seems connected to this vision. The car is black or dark in color, possibly blue." The family discussed a number of possibilities but no one divined any special meaning and all wondered why this vision kept appearing to me. Tony kept bringing it up over and over, until it became not only an annoyance, but a source of real frustration for all involved. I explained that when Spirit brings up something repeatedly, it means one of two things for me: I either haven't given the information correctly or I'm spot on and the family hasn't figured it out yet. Tony finally gave up and we continued with the remainder of the reading, after which the family of three left. Less than five minutes later my doorbell rang and there stood Greg, Tony's brother-in-law. He had this quirky smile on his face and said, "Janet, my car won't start." Thinking nothing of it, of course I offered to help. I walked out the door and turned to where his car was parked and the surprise on my face must have been comical. There sat his car, at the end of the street, with the hood up. His car is black. The battery was dead. I just shook my head and smiled. We now finally understood what Tony was trying to tell us—I bet he found

123

our situation entertaining. As I went to get my car so Greg could connect the jumper cables, I thought to myself that sometimes it's the smallest of details. I smile every time I think about this story and how Tony just wanted to give us a heads up.

***

Messages from spirit come through in many forms and it can be disheartening when someone believes their loved one can come through only in a specific way. Based on long experience, I know they will come through however they are able to and whenever a moment is available. They will do their best to get through, but it's up to you to stay open and not disregard a flickering light, a voice in the night, a tug on a sleeve or a dead battery. I'm not asking you to believe anything and everything, I simply ask you to be open to possibilities.

***

Grandma Helen

Sitting in my great room one afternoon relaxing, a vision of my grandma Helen suddenly appeared. Standing in the doorway to the kitchen, she was wearing a dress with multiples of tiny flowers scattered across it billowing in the nonexistent breeze. She stood there, fingers entwined together, silently watching me as if this were nothing out of the ordinary. Considering it's been over twenty years since I last saw her, I immediately perked up with excitement, wanting to know what she was about to show me. My delight was tempered as I felt a warning extend from her, becoming stronger until I felt an alarming sense of dread. I could feel the panic rise up around me, then as she faded out I saw a vision of the church she belonged to while living here on earth. At the front of the altar, in the aisle was a body on a gurney with a sheet covering part of it. I saw the toes sticking out and a tag wrapped around the big toe. I suddenly realized this was connected to my brother in some way and I became frightened while tears spilled down my cheek. "Why did she stop by to show me this?" I wondered. I may be a psychic medium but I'm also human and an emotional one at that. Pulling myself together, I knew she was trying to help me in some way with this vision. This is the way it works, I know, so I knew enough to take action.

I immediately called my brother to tell him Grandma Helen stopped by, and proceeded to explain what she showed me and that it related directly to him. I told him not to freak out, that I didn't believe it was him, rather someone else around him. By now, my brother was used to my visions and so I knew he would understand my concern. I felt Grandma wanted to prepare him. Not surprisingly my brother informed me that his friend Brett, who we both knew, was in emergency surgery that day, most likely at that very moment. I hoped my interpretation was off and I had the situation wrong. Maybe Grandma Helen wanted my brother and me to pray for Brett while in surgery and so we did.

Later that day, my brother called to tell me Brett stopped breathing while in surgery and that his brain had flat-lined for a couple of minutes. The doctors revived him and Brett survived although with some complications, so he is taking life one day at a time. Hanging up the phone, I sat and thought about what Grandma Helen showed me. She was warning us to be prepared that the situation wasn't going to turn out as we anticipated. I realized she had given us a heads up. Although it didn't affect my daily life, it had an impact to someone I loved, my brother and those connected to him. By showing him in a church she was asking us to pray for him, and I believe our prayers helped. Prayers are positive energy, and anytime you send someone positive energy I believe it goes to a deep cellular level, a place of healing. I also believe Grandma Helen was there to give support to him as well.

I've learned over the course of my life that the visions I see aren't always things I wish to see, but by seeing them, I'm given a purpose: to let others know death isn't an end but a transition. Our loved ones may leave their body, but will continue to live in Spirit.

We see tragic and painful endings from our side, but most people never get to see what's on the other side. If I can show you what I witness through my abilities and what Spirit brings me, I'm giving a gift I hope will offer a little peace. I've struggled for so many years with seeing death, only to find my fears have been eliminated through awareness of my visions. I've seen loved ones and friends come through looking happy, normal, even better than normal. Dwelling on how you lost them or how they looked before they passed doesn't change the facts. Remember the life they lived while here and all the goodness you were able to share with them. Continue to celebrate their life with memories and a will to live that is stronger for having known them. I learned many lessons from my grandma that day. She reminded me to accept what I see and maintain the positive perspective. I learn from each vision I experience, live with it, but more importantly, accept it.

***

A Starry Night

A couple of months ago I planned lunch with girlfriends I hadn't seen in a while—I'd known Ruthie since high school, and I'd met Angie through a reading I'd done for her months earlier. At that time, I found out she also happens to be friends with Ruthie through their sons' school. They have both lost a number of loved ones and one of Ruthie's deceased relatives dropped in on me with a surprise visit. I was looking forward to sharing with Ruthie what I had received, and I also wanted to see if anyone would come through for Angie who had several times said she would love another connection. Sitting down, I asked if her dad or brother had anything they wanted to show me that I could share with her. I never know if someone will come through or not, so I was surprised by the vision that quickly emerged. I watched as Angie's brother Tony began scribbling back and forth quickly across invisible paper, as if drawing or creating some type of art work. It was immediately impressed upon my mind that this somehow related to Angie's oldest son, Dominic. I wasn't sure how, since I had never met Dominic. Furthermore, I felt that this vision somehow related to Tony as well. It felt like the two had a common connection through art.

I explained this to Angie later that day at lunch. She said she knew exactly what Tony was referring to, and went on to explain that Dominic had a piece of his artwork on display at the local mall. Angie and her husband were so proud of him that they even brought the grandparents to see it. He created a picture in art class where he took a print of Vincent van Gogh's, *Starry Night* and added two other pieces of famous art work combined together to make a new picture. Tony loved *Starry Night*, as well as Vincent van Gogh. So the picture Dominic created did correlate with Tony, because while Tony was here on earth, he had a framed print of *Starry Night* hanging on the wall in his apartment.

The story did not end there. When Angie returned home after lunch that day she called her mom to tell her what had transpired. They began talking and Angie wondered where that picture was. The art fair was over some weeks before and she hasn't seen it since. She no sooner said that to her mom, when the door opened, and in walked the kids home from school. Dominic was holding that picture in his hand, facing toward Angie. She said the hair on her arms stood up and she began to cry. She later stated in an email: Janet, you clarified that Tony came to you that morning, which told me he possibly saw Dominic with that picture at school that day. I don't know the details of his "viewing" with us, but I am completely convinced that he's around us and that he saw my son's artwork. You have helped us come to terms with our losses and find a place of peace in our hearts because of your abilities. Your reminders are a blessing!

***

As mentioned, every reading delves into the sitter's family history, including all the intricate twists and turns of their life. Throughout this chapter I continue to present many such twists, as well as presenting some clients' reactions they generously offered to share. Some chose to email a list of validations along with their stories, yet others jotted mini-accounts. Although most accounts were written at the time of their reading, others were written within weeks, months, or even years afterwards. Their wish is that those who are drawn to this book will find some peace through their own reading as well as their own personal experiences which we can all learn from.

Kimberly

This next story is of course different than the previous stories shared in this chapter. I chose to help share another's important message that needs to be conveyed in addition to my own. This not only tells the tale of a man's love toward his wife, but for the gift he brings to others because of that love. It is truly a story of how the human heart is never bound by time and space and can change the lives of many.

Our lives can be cut short in the blink of an eye. We really don't know how long we have, so we need to live our lives with as much purpose and love as possible. Kim was one of those purposeful and loving spirits. She had a zest for life and gave so much to her husband, kids, family and friends. She was not only intelligent, but beautiful inside and out. When Kim first came through I immediately felt her smiling, and her sense of humor that was goofy and fun loving. It was as if her energy was bouncing off the walls. It's always validating to see a spirit come through in this way, showing how we continue to hold on to these qualities even when we have left our body. This means our Spirit continues to live on as we know it.

Kim's husband, Mike, came to me searching for a connection with "his baby," who was the light of his world. To everyone around her, Kim was a neon light in a world of 40-watt incandescent bulbs. Mike desperately needed some type of validation that she lives on, is in peace and is watching over her family. He was hopeful that she'd seen the positive changes he and her family had made in her name.

I appreciate that Mike has been kind enough to share parts of his reading. He said there were 62 total observations, and the ones he wanted to share are presented here due to their personal significance and validating content.

Kim first showed shoes, sandals or no shoes relating to her funeral. She was adamant about bringing up this issue to Mike, so much so that I repeated it a number of times. Mike explained this was a huge validation because only the funeral director, their friend, Jessilyn, and himself knew about the shoe issue. After Jessilyn dressed Kim's body and did her hair, the funeral director wanted to put Kim in the coffin without shoes. Jessilyn pitched a fit and told him there was no way she was going to let her go anywhere without her heels. Only the shoes would complete her silky gold outfit Mike chose for her to wear and she knew Kim wouldn't go anywhere without wearing shoes. She further went on to tell the funeral director that Kim would haunt her if she didn't make sure she had them on in her coffin! Jessilyn made them wait on her while she went out and bought Kim some shoes to match the gold outfit. Mike felt this is what Kim was trying to share, mainly because he had forgotten about this until it was mentioned in the reading. He felt that Kim knew this would be the most credible validation from her because no one in the general public would know about it.

Being shown next was a boy on the other side who was in Kim's life, and who passed at an early age of twelve or thirteen. He was there to greet her, along with the two women described earlier in the reading. Mike explained that the little boy was Kim's cousin, Michael, who had passed away at age twelve. They were very close and their seven-year-old son Connor Michael is named after him. Mike thought the two women were possibly his mother and definitely his Aunt Marg, because the latter's name was mentioned later in the reading.

Staying open to what comes through can often bring humor. In Mike's case, two older women were showing Mike an incident with frogs. Not having any other direction to go with this vision, I asked Mike if he has ever eaten frog legs. Mike replied after the reading, "When I was a child and after my brothers and I had gigged some frogs, my mom began to fry the legs for us to eat. They started jumping in the pan and my mom freaked out and yelled for my Dad to come kill the frogs because they were jumping in the skillet and still alive!" Mike said there was no way I could have generally or randomly guessed at this. I felt his Mom wanted to give him validation with a touch of humor to make him smile and remember good times.

Kim popped back in with a song, however it felt like a song she or Mike made up and related to their kids. I knew it was made up, because I also made up songs for my son and she brought those songs of mine up. She's clever! Mike shared that Kim used to sing to Chloe and Connor whenever she walked into their rooms, to get them out of their cribs. "What are you doin'? What are you doin'?" she would sing in a baby voice while dancing to their cribs. Mike explained this was very, very cute and Chloe would laugh and grin every single time she did it!

I felt a tap, a feather-light tickle on my left shoulder, ear and in-between. Mike informed me that after Kim passed, for months he felt a buzzing sensation in his left ear as if someone were whispering in it, like a sense of someone blowing in his ear. When he said this, I felt it was a validation that Kim was letting us know she was still near.

Kim impressed upon me a D name and it felt like a nickname for her. A nickname can just about be anything. I made a couple of stabs at names, but they didn't feel right. I kept writing D, D, D, then finally I was shown something specific and I came up with "Daisy."

Mike confirmed the Daisy was Kim's symbol and that she had a daisy tattoo on her pelvis. A shiver ran down my spine as things suddenly clicked in my mind: "Oh my gosh, she's the daisy person?" I went on to explain how a "daisy person" had been contacting me for at least a month before Mike contacted me. Kim already knew or was directing Mike my way. It was at this point I mentioned how a teen boy in Spirit, who I knew from a previous reading months earlier came to me and told me that a family was going to contact me within a day or so and they needed my help. This young man had only come to me one other time. I knew to heed his advice, because if someone was coming from the other side to bring me this news, I better pay attention. Sure enough, Mike emailed me a day later.

Kim showed a woman's name, Kelly, and then a big OK filtered across my vision, then this scenario was repeated. Kim wanted to make sure this information got mentioned. Hearing names from the other side is difficult, so when one does emerge with such force and repetitiveness, I knew I had to mention it. In this case, Kim wanted to get across to Kelly that she was OK! Mike was not surprised by Kim's concern. Kelly was Kim's best friend and she was pregnant at the time of the reading.

The only numbers Kim showed during the entire reading were numbers that looked like: 256, 257, 267.

Mike explained Kim's birthday was 2/6/75.

The other number she gave was three. Kim impressed three of something and I didn't think it was children because I was only seeing two small children. Every time I sat down to meditate she showed three fingers. Mike knew exactly what Kim was talking about and cleared up my confusion immediately. He explained that she held up three fingers, waving me off when I mentioned two, because she considered Nathan, her step-son, as her own child. She along with Mike fought very hard to gain custody of him. Mike said she was always so proud to hold up those three fingers. While meditating I kept seeing two children, but three fingers. I didn't think there was one on the way at the time of her passing. It was more definite in the way I was receiving this. When I "asked" for more information, Kim would shake her head and wave her hand as if to say: No, no, no, Janet! And then hold up three fingers again. Once I wrote down three instead of two, we moved on. Kim would often shake her head if I was slow on picking up something she was trying to convey. She even placed her hands on her hips in mock disbelief and shook her head as if to say: Come on! Get with the picture, girl! As you can see, some spirits can be quite demanding. They will keep pushing until you figure it out or until they are happy with the outcome. Personalities stay with the person, and Kim knew she could give me a hard time and I would keep at it. Just as my first impression of her came through, I guess mine came through to her as well. Kim and I seemed to have hit it off.

Kim kept showing a birthday cake. She wanted me to acknowledge this birthday and the cake. Mike's voice held tears as he shared that Kim passed away six days before her daughter Chloe's second birthday. She had previously organized everything for the party. The day of the party, the petting zoo, banners, and other decorations were all delivered to their home just as she arranged. Kim's mom made a cake especially for Chloe "from Mommy" and it's this cake he felt Kim was showing.

All my readings hold great importance to me on many levels. I am responsible for sharing a message from the other side, as well as keeping it "clean" in the sense I share the way they come though, feelings and all. I am just the vessel through which the message travels. Kim came through so strongly to me that I had to stop a number of times throughout the reading. Finding myself in tears a number of times during the meditation showed the intense emotion she sent to me. When the meditation was over, I felt as if I lost a loved one as well. The overwhelming love for her family was constantly impressed upon me. I usually place my emotions to one side during the reading, but it was not possible when Kim came through. When I found myself talking to Mike for the first time, it was quite unusual in one sense. Kim placed me in her life in order to show me the overwhelming love she shared with Mike and her kids. Not wanting to sound invasive about his personal life, I had to share the feelings she impressed on me, letting Mike know I felt their love for each other and their family was an extremely strong bond, one that even time and space couldn't dissolve. Mike was grateful I shared this and was surprisingly open to what I said. He knew that the love he shared with Kim was strong and special and not to be taken for granted. He was pleased that Kim showed me what it was like. It was a gift.

Last, Kim kept showing an ATM machine with a panic button and I asked Mike if he could relate to this. It turns out that Kim was showing that Mike has gone above and beyond what she would ever have imagined someone would do for her out of love. She showed me that he would be doing more in the future pertaining to this and safety. Curious, at the end of the reading I asked Mike about this vision. Once he explained what he was doing, I was amazed at the tribute to Kim's memory and the personal task he had committed himself to in order to help others.

Kim passed away on September 12, 2005, leaving a huge gap in Mike's heart and in his world. Mike could have lived within that pain, and everyone would have understood and continued to give comfort and support. However, Mike knew Kim had given him a serious and substantial job that he couldn't just allow to pass by—it was too serious a matter.

Kim had hopped into her car, drove to work, once there she took one of the rental trucks to get gas, then headed back to work where she was abducted in front of the business that she and Mike owned. She got back a little later than usual. A convicted rapist, child molester, armed robber and non-registered sex offender who had just been released from jail three months earlier had crossed Kim's path. He traveled two states and ended up in Kim's neck of the woods. Some would claim she was in the wrong place at the wrong time. Because of the many readings I do, I see things differently, and felt Kim was where she was supposed to be—it was the actions of many others, not only Kim that brought this about. She was forced at gun point to go to an ATM machine and withdraw money. Somehow she was able to go to one closer to her home, hoping someone may recognize her. The ATM camera caught her on tape, yet she had no way to sound an alarm about the situation she was currently in. The cameras are only recorders to see past transactions. If only they had humans on the other side on constant watch, this story may never have needed to be told. Three feet away was a teller window, but it must have seemed like hundreds of feet away to Kim. There was no way to alert the police or even the bank of an ATM robbery that was currently taking place. She was in trouble and ATM machines have no panic button or way to alert others. She was in a situation that no one could have imagined.

After leaving the ATM she began to drive erratically, hoping to upset the man with the gun enough to save herself. A witness saw what was happening and began to follow her. Kim was able to stop the car once and attempted to jump out, only to be pulled back in and forced to continue driving. She clawed, swinging her arms in hopes of upsetting the man and his gun. She was shot in the side after crossing the bridge which caused her vehicle to slam into the guard rail. Hoping for a chance to escape, she continued to struggle, and even tried to climb out the window, only to be pulled back in. A witness saw the man push her in the back and then take over driving and yet Kim continued her fight. Attempting to beat a cement truck through an intersection, he was hit by it instead. Jumping out with Kim's purse in hand, he ran. The witness who saw what happened called out to him to stop. The robber turned on him. The witness, a licensed gun carrier took aim and yelled once again for the man to stop. The robber turned and pointed his gun. It was then the witness fired his licensed gun three times, killing the convicted rapist, robber, and sex-offender. The witness quickly ran to the car hoping to help Kim. It was too late.

Kim, a beautiful soul, a wife, mother and friend was taken from the lives of her loved ones. Mike, taking into consideration Kim's situation, along with her strength, passion and the love they shared made a difference. He knew that he didn't ever want someone else's loved ones to have to experience what Kim and her family had to live through. Mike has allowed me to share what he has accomplished, below, so I can help him in making a difference as well. This is what you will find on "The Kimberly Boyd Legacy" website:

Accomplishments This 2006 Legislative Session

After several meetings with the Georgia Department of Corrections in which we discussed the releasing policies and procedures involving sex offenders, a 4-step process was changed to a 9-step process. The 9-step process now includes checking the background history of inmates due to be released and also checking the systems for any arrest warrants from all law enforcement agencies. Both of which were not a part of standard procedure before September 12, 2005. Other changes include the methods used to notify probation officers, district attorneys, and sheriff departments. There will be no more regular-mail notification attempts to probation officers. Now they will be notified by email, or by fax if no email is available. Confirmation of notification must be received or there is a follow up phone call. The notification attempt has to be confirmed in order for there to be considered an official notification. Before, only an effort to notify was sufficient. Email will also be used to notify DAs and sheriff departments unless email is not available and then, again, fax will be used followed by a phone call if no confirmation is received. Proper notification to the probation officer in June when this sex-offender was released would have saved my wife's life.

- House Bill 1059 was passed by both the Senate and House sides of the General Assembly and will be signed into law on Wednesday, April 26, 2006. This new law introduces minimum mandatory sentences and review boards that will determine which sex offenders are dangerous sexual predators. Once a sex offender is deemed a sexual predator, he/she will have to wear a GPS tracking system the rest of his/her life. This law also mandates that all sex offenders being released will have to be registered before leaving prison and they also are restricted from living, working, or loitering near anywhere kids may be gathering. This law, along with the procedural changes of the DOC, will significantly reduce the chances of any more offenders falling through gaping holes in the judicial and correction systems. Proper registration and tracking of them would have saved Kimberly's life. Less judicial discretion would have saved Kimberly's life.

All states need to acquire stricter and tougher sex-offender laws.

- The "Kimberly's Call" was also introduced and passed in the General Assembly this session. This addition to the "Levi's Call" originated from the awareness that not only did society need to help police in locating fugitives of child related crimes, but also the harsh reality that society needs to also help police locate fugitives who have committed violent crimes against women, mothers, men, and fathers. Now when there is a violent crime committed against an adult where the person is either abducted, raped, murdered, or otherwise in imminent danger, and there is enough information available for the public to assist in finding the fugitive (i.e., make and model of the vehicle, plate number, partial or whole description of the suspect), the Department of Transportation will issue an alert that will be broadcasted across radio, television, and interstate signs to be on the look out for the violent suspect. Now not only will children have a fighting chance when abducted or in imminent danger, but so will their mothers and fathers. Had the DOT issued a Kimberly's Call on September 6, 2005 after her offender had brutally abducted, beaten, and raped the other Acworth lady and escaped in her car, the public would have seen him trying to ditch the car at the busy North Metro Tech University and someone would have called the police and Kimberly would be alive today.

I hope that everyone will take some time and help support this needed change in your state. Each state should have an alert for adults, as well as children.

- The Allatoona Lake Bridge north of the Lake Acworth Drive and

Highway 41 intersection will now be named "The Kimberly Boyd Memorial Bridge." Senate Resolution 849 unanimously passed both the Senate and the House sides of the General Assembly to name this bridge after Kimberly. This bridge is the same bridge where she fought for her life, and her family's and anyone else's who might have been harmed if she had chosen to be a passive victim. Instead, she showed heroic courage and determination in making sure that everyone on the road that morning knew there was a rapist, child molester, and murderer in her car trying to attack and escape again like he had done the week before. This is a small but very appreciated token of gratitude shown by the state of Georgia that we hope will show to Kimberly's children the kind of woman that was taken from their young lives.

- Senate Bills 379 and 513 were referred to subcommittees for study over the summer. This is a small step toward getting these bills voted on and passed in the next session in January of 2007. Of all of the actions we set out to accomplish after Kimberly's death, one would think that proposals to make ATM's safer to use by having 911 buttons and a reverse pin code to activate when in danger and being forced to withdraw money, would have been the easiest to accomplish. After all, both ideas originate from common sense and everyone recognizes the need for the safety features on ATMs, but ironically and tragically this is not the case. Due to objections from the Banking Associations and a host of excuses to not implement common-sense safety devices, these associations have successfully stalled the progress of these life-saving features. But with a little more time and pressure from the public, who is becoming more and more informed on the dangers of ATM use and the criminal element who preys on people using ATMs, it is just a matter of time when the Banking Association will have to take action and be forced to be more concerned about human life and less concerned about budgets and bottom lines. Had these safety features been in place on September 6, 2005 or September 12, 2005, Kimberly would be alive today.

Update-The senate committee met and found that there was enough available information to warrant further safety precautions at ATMs, but they also said that they needed more information and at this time the bills are still sitting in the senate. The sponsors of the bills say they do not have enough support from their fellow legislators in the Banking and Financial Institutions Committee to get the bill passed out of committee and to the senate floor. Banking Association's lobbyists are paid to hound these legislators daily during the general assembly to make sure they don't pass safety bills that will cost their corporate sponsor's money. While Mike spoke to this committee on behalf of Kim and the safety features, there were 12 lobbyists waiting their turn to speak against making ATMs safer.

Please join me in helping Mike and many others by demanding stricter sex offender protocol and policies in each state, as well as changing the ATM laws. If everyone would be more aware of ATM safety in their state or community we could make a difference. This would force those who hold power to listen. Contact your local senators and congressmen and express the urgency in getting these objectives passed through as law. It may save your loved one.

At Your Service!

When Valerie came to me for a reading she had a number of family and friends drop in to make their presence known. Not that this is unusual for me to have so many come through, but what I found so exciting was the fact that the messages they gave were incredibly clear. Her friends and loved ones were not only ready and waiting, they were on speaker phone!

Below, Valerie shares parts of her reading that gave her even more validation about the afterlife than she'd had before. I wanted to share this to let you know how often during a reading someone receives information they didn't know or that hasn't happened as of yet. When this occurs, I remind the client to be open and patient—the situation will often play out over time.

Valerie writes:

The first person to come through in my reading was my father. That was quite clear. You said the man was smiling, did not have much hair, had passed from lung cancer and was saying "At Your Service." My ex-husband and I owned a business after my father died from lung cancer, called "At Your Service." My mother came through as a quiet and reserved woman, who passed from respiratory illness. She wasn't sure she should be there, something she portrayed in life as well. She always felt like a guest, and although there was plenty of love she could never quite feel at home anywhere but her own place. She was holding a black-and-white cat. Well that was my mom, and the day my mom died from respiratory illness, my black-and-white cat also died.

My dear friend Gloria came through too. You mentioned a passing quite awhile ago from a car accident and that this energy was making you laugh, that she was very funny. Gloria was the funniest person I have ever known. She was laughing about who was coming through next, which turned out to be my late mother-in-law. You not only described my late mother-in-law perfectly as someone who loved to cook (not bake), and was a loud and very boisterous person, you also said she was connected to someone who "made a record or wrote a song, had something to do with music." My husband was a musician and recorded a record in the 1960s. You also mentioned the name "George," which was my husband's brother who was in a nursing home at the time of the reading.

Another startling part of the reading was when you talked about, "a police officer coming through, a thirty-six or thirty-seven-year-old young male—distant, northern feel to the energy; showing much remorse for his actions, something he did—behind him was a fire truck and an ambulance; he wanted to send a hug to a child, he was showing intense remorse." He was saying "I was in the kitchen when something broke, I was there, I'm always there in the kitchen with you, I am so sorry." I knew immediately who this was, and that it didn't relate to me, as there are no police officers in my family. A friend of mine lost her son just four months before the reading. He was indeed from up north, he was thirty seven years old, and a police officer. He was going through a difficult divorce and unfortunately killed his ex-wife and then himself, leaving behind a seven-year-old child. At the time of the reading my friend was in Arizona on vacation, she called me after the reading to see how it went. I didn't know if I should tell her about her son coming through, because I didn't know if she would believe me, but I decided I would. She listened and then I could hear her cry, and she hung up on me. An hour later she called back to say she was sorry, but when I said "he was in the kitchen when something broke," she knew without a doubt her son had come through. Unknown to me, the day before she left, she was in the kitchen and broke a vase her son had given her, she sat on the floor and cried, saying "why did I have to break this of all things?" She also said when her son was alive, he would always spend time in the kitchen with her. He loved to cook.

Earlier in the reading you mentioned you saw "butter." You thought this would relate to the name, "Parkay." You kept seeing butter, and weren't sure what this meant! Well, my friend's other son, lives in Land O' Lakes, Florida. Even I didn't know this. I thought he lived in Tampa. Everything in the reading with the exception of two or three things were validated. The above, to me, was the most startling and unexpected.

***

Almost every client of mine has had at least one psychic instance—a vision, a dream, a feeling of presence or a manifestation of an everyday item sent from a loved one. Go ahead, call that penny that seemingly dropped from the sky, or a feather that suddenly appeared on the table a "coincidence." Now, stop and think about it, they are small and almost weightless. I believe it takes a combination of energy, theirs and ours to bring about the conditions needed to make something so seemingly minute, into something so unbelievably important. Isn't it to our benefit to at least say "Thanks?"

In My Mind, I'm Goin' to Carolina...

Janet did my reading in August of 2009. I was amazed from the very beginning. I had requested assistance from my guides regarding certain issues and had made a list of questions. Though I didn't share the list with Janet, she proceeded with the reading in exactly the order of my list. Although most of the reading was personal, I wanted to share a couple synchronicities that suggest the existence of a father's concern even after physical death.

Throughout the reading, Janet kept mentioning a man who was present. She said he smoked either a cigar or pipe, not cigarettes, and that he wore a plaid shirt and somewhat high-waist pants. She said that he was pointing to his heart. I thought it could be my dad, who had died of a heart attack when I was nineteen, but the connection wasn't clear because my dad *never* wore plaid shirts. Janet then described that he was doing something kind of strange with the hair above his forehead, as if it "does something funny or sticks out there." I was confused by this description until I remembered a picture I had of my dad wearing a plaid poncho my mom has made for me (he was being silly). Then I remembered the hairdo I had created for my dad: I used to comb it down into a point on his forehead! Yes. That was certainly my dad who was giving me the message through Janet; he was "there for me now."

A somewhat surprising and amusing event occurred months after the reading. Janet told me that at one point her left wrist was hurting and that whenever that type of thing happened, it usually was related to the person she was reading. She then said that she was getting the message "Going to Carolina." She received no more information and told me that sometimes these things made sense later. Three months later, I was having outpatient surgery; they had just finished putting in an IV line in my left arm just above the wrist. It was hurting badly when the anesthesiologist came into the room singing the line from a James Taylor song, *"In my mind I'm goin' to Carolina."* What a strange but wonderful verification that my guides and those on the other side are watching over me!

When Christine shared this validation it reminded me of years before when I had an outpatient procedure. My sister drove me there, since my procedure required a general anesthetic. When I came to, my sister was sitting by my side and the first thing she said was, "You just freaked out the nurse."

"How did I do that?" I asked.

"When you first came to, you told everyone that you were talking to John Denver. The nurse commented that patients make odd statements, however that wasn't what did it. When you were wheeled into this room, the first song we heard was John Denver singing *Rocky Mountain High*. The nurse heard it and said, "That's it, I'm outta here!""

I smiled. I don't remember if I spoke with John Denver or not, but found it apropos considering my life, especially since he had died many years before.

Kristen's Reunion

For private readings, I always make a list of what I see and I write up my reading beforehand while in my meditation. I talk through the majority of the reading, due to the number of pages of notes I wrote during the meditations. My readings are like putting the pieces of a puzzle together—each time I meditate a little more is revealed. The reason I meditate at least two or three days for a reading is because I feel we can all have an off day. My method allows me to get different messages on different days, which forms a more complete picture for the client. Each reading is as unique as each human being. At first, I wasn't planning to share so much of Kristen's reading. Like the others, the individual stories I felt would offer a variety of issues and angles. However, after receiving her email, I decided that by sharing most of the reading, you will have the opportunity to walk through someone else's life and experience their personal messages and gifts they receive from the other side.

Background to the validation given by Kristen:

My brother David Brian passed away in January 2005 in a car accident. He was drinking or high at the time. A bottle of liquor called "Hot Damn" was found under the car seat. His four-year-old son Michael Brian was in a car seat in the back. My brother was a machinist who wore jeans and plaid shirts, an extremely intelligent man who did not finish school. He always carried a laminated driver's license size copy of his GED in his wallet. He dreamed of our late grandmother the night before he died and told his wife, the morning of the accident, that he felt like he was going to die. She reassured him that he was probably just stressed over his job. He and his wife were at odds when he died and he knew I thought she was right and he was wrong. His most horrific and probably fatal injury was to the right side of his skull. All I had, of his, at the time of the reading was a box of papers of his clippings, cards, old magazines and so on. A soldier from our grandmother's hometown in another state happened to be passing on the same rural road at the time of the accident. He used a pocket knife to cut my nephew out of his car seat and stayed with my nephew until help came. I viewed the body at the funeral home for peace of mind or some sort of closure.

Validations:
- You got the name Brian
- He died from odd /unusual circumstance and he knew it
- Before he passed he knew
- 911 was called
- We had papers connecting us
- He was showing you a small card the size of a driver's license but not a driver's license

- He told you he was smart
- He told you he improved something
- He visited once in the kitchen
- Stressed something about the sink/water running
- You saw metal parts connected to him or his job
- You saw jeans and plaid shirts
- He had a sick feeling before passing
- Alcohol or meds were in his system but he was hesitant to share this and would only go so far
- There was a burning inside him at the time
- There was an explosion from within
- He wanted to thank a military guy on the scene
- He's "here" and he's good
- Didn't feel good but he got over it
- Held his arms out as if to say, "See, I'm better now."
- Someone was mad at him or he was mad at somebody but it doesn't matter now
- He is taking responsibility for contributing to his own passing
- He is saying, "Let it go. It doesn't matter anymore."
- He is watching over them (outside of me)
- He put his hand over his head as a gesture or as a way of covering up an injury location as if to say, "Sorry you had to see that."

You said he had visited once in kitchen or near running water (4 months later I was going through his things and had them spread out on the kitchen counter and suddenly felt his presence when my aunt turned on the water)

Spirit Two: Kristen's Grandmother

Background:

My grandmother died at the age of 62 of brain cancer that slowly took away her speech and then her mobility. She separately and simultaneously had breast cancer but died from brain cancer. We were very close. Her mother died when she was only five. I dreamed she got out of the wheelchair and danced with me in her kitchen. On the back of her funeral program we printed the lyrics to "I Hope You Dance." Her name was Ina. She was a cool grandma who never let herself go gray and always had wavy brown hair.

Validations:
You said
- She had wavy hair
- She was older but not old-fashioned
- She showed you a foot or leg issue
- Put her hand on chest indicating breast cancer or heart trouble
- You got a "na" name
- She showed you her nice legs
- Made a connection to dancing

Spirit Three: Kristen's Great Grandmother

My great grandmother, Ina's mother, died when Ina was only five.

Validations:
You said
- This spirit was in position to be a generation older than my grandmother but looked younger

Spirit Four: Kristen's Grandfather

Validations:
You said loosely
- He smoked a pipe (I did have a grandpa who regularly smoked a pipe)
- He lived on the land (the same grandpa had lumber mills)
- He had lung cancer or covered his chest indicative of lung cancer (this same grandfather did die of lung cancer)
- He wore a hat (he did, a fedora type)
- He was medium to large build (he was)

Spirit Five: A.T.

You said a minister was coming through, "a holy man to watch out for you."

Validation:
There was a minister and his wife, who often babysat my brother and I when we were little and were close to our family.

Spirit 6: Kim

- You said Kim and I were both there in this image and she had a huge (massive/bigger than a person) bouquet of white flowers. We were dressed as brides and she was passing the flowers to me in a passing of the torch kind of way.
- She has visited my dreams.
- You said that she sort of took over your writing and wrote that the children were not her kids but our kids. You said there were children with her on the other side who were not her family. There was a new baby with her. She is proud of me and thanks me. She comes to me at night. If the children are sick she will help but she will leave me alone and hopes I like the new place (we redid a lot of the house). She mentioned wrought iron (We did move a huge wrought iron piece that had hung above the mantle). She wants me to know she is distant and "knows her place".
- You asked what happened to Mike's pants. We had not been able to find pairs of his pants off and on for awhile. We would fold them and put them away and then they'd be gone.

Miscellaneous Information
- You said my dreams can show the future and loved ones.

I have dreams, from time to time, about things as they happen.

A few examples:

I dreamed about a former boyfriend with a round gunshot wound in the back of his head. Turns out he had been gun shopping in another country to commit suicide at the exact time I dreamed it. I had lost touch with him and had no idea he was suicidal.

While living in Korea, near China, I dreamed that I was running and the ground was splitting open behind me. I could barely outrun it. I later found out that an earthquake had happened in China at the time I had the dream.

I dreamed I was floating on a piece of debris from a shipwreck and other people were too. All of the other people looked Asian. I later found out via Yahoo news that there was a major passenger ship wreck in the Philippines.

- In my reading you asked if I was a bad cook or if I had ever burned anything in the kitchen. There was a burning in the kitchen according to the reading. I couldn't make a connection to that until 4 months later.

- You said I had a job "switch" coming up that was school related. (Thanks to the budget cuts I do indeed have a change coming up.)

- You said there were two boys together. (One of the biggest stories in my family is that of my grandpa's two brothers who died as children walking across a dam to take their dad lunch. The younger one slipped and the older one grabbed his hand. They both drowned and when they were found, they were still holding hands.

- The spirits showed me with a digestive trouble "eating then not feeling good" in the past. (I vacationed in the Philippines and got very ill. They thought I had malaria. I could not get a cab to the airport in the middle of the night with a high fever. I was scared and miserable. I think this meant they were with me at that trying time.)

I felt this reading was important to share for a number of reasons. Words we hear so often that they become a mainstream phrase are, "Don't drink and drive." Unfortunately David put himself and his son at risk. It is a blessing, through the chain of events that emerged, that his son was saved. On any given day anyone can make a bad choice. We are after all, human. If this story can make one person pay attention to their daily actions, then this story is a gift from David, his family and Kristen. Not everyone is given a second chance. This life isn't just a day-to-day grind, it's an opportunity. Make the best of it.

Another important part to this reading is that Kristen learned information about loved ones and the future while in a dream state. Kristen could verify what was given to me because she was aware of it already. In Kristen's case it was nice to have a "second opinion" that she was already getting valid information through dreams. The reading acknowledged that she has gifts of her own that she can use and develop to an even-greater extent in her daily life. It's really exciting when clients share their personal stories. I feel it's a gift to humanity for everyone to know they can experience their own personal spiritual growth. If you personally feel you receive information from a loved one, acknowledge it and accept it for the message it brings. I always feel that such an event opens the door, allowing for more of the same.

Sherry's Thoughts

I first went to Janet for a reading in April 2005. Although I did not know it at the time, the next several years would bring major personal losses, including my mother and husband. I now believe I was drawn to Janet at that time for a reason. I had previously been to only two mediums in my life (both when I was very young); and since I am a professor, I am trained to be skeptical about matters of proof. So when I decided to seek out a medium, I did some research, which led me to the University of Arizona HESL experiments. In those experiments, Janet was one of a notable few who were able to demonstrate a high level of accuracy. Also, when I went to her website, I was drawn to the simplicity and sense of authenticity to the presentation—characteristics that I would come to admire in her person. So I will describe a few points from past readings between 2005 and 2009, which she could not have known without some visitation or psychic awareness.

First and most significant was the vision of my husband's bladder cancer. When Janet first told me in 2005 that my husband had a "bladder problem," I discounted the comment. In fact, I told her that I thought the comment might pertain to me as I have periodic urinary infections. She didn't respond. It was not until several months later that we learned my husband had an advanced case of bladder cancer, from which he died two-and-a-half years later. Over the course of several readings, I found that Janet was particularly good at identifying medical issues. For example, she told me that my daughter has a lot of problems with her stomach. This is very true. We have even taken her to the emergency room on occasion because she doubles over with pain; and despite extensive testing, they have never identified the problem. Janet also told me that a close member of my family had had colon cancer. That was also true. She told me I had a problem with my right ear. In fact, I sleep with a bottle of antibiotic ear drops beside my bed. I have extreme problems with my right ear, which I attribute to allergies, although I have never understood why I don't have the same problems with my left ear. To her credit, Janet was always careful, when speaking of medical issues, to couch the information in terms that would generate awareness but not fear. She reminded me that she wasn't a physician and never made a diagnosis; she simply said what she saw or what those on the other side shared with her. She always encouraged me to remember to have a yearly physical.

Sometimes the information from the readings brought smiles. In the first reading, Janet told me she saw someone who looked like Abe Lincoln. She saw him wearing a plaid shirt, which she associated with manual labor and wood. Immediately I identified the man as my deceased father, who was a construction worker. His favorite shirts were plaid. This information does not appear anywhere on the Internet, and a funny story goes with the reference to Abe Lincoln. My father was tall and lean with straight black hair, associated with a native connection. On one occasion, he had gone to a little store near our home called Abe's Grocery to pick up a few items for my mother. After he left, my mother called the store to ask him to add another item to the list. When asked for some physical description, my mother said, "He looks like Abe Lincoln!" Although my father didn't look like Abe Lincoln in terms of specifics, he had his build and black hair and coloring. So Janet's reference to *Abe Lincoln* particularly resonated—both in terms of the name of the store and the incident with my father.

On another occasion, Janet referenced a time years ago involving a swimsuit incident with my mother. She mentioned my mother was groaning and laughing about a swimsuit. My mother and I had gone to Virginia Beach about 40 years ago. She couldn't find any swimsuits except for a two-piece, which she purchased. She had reservations about how she looked in it but concluded, "Oh well, we won't see anyone of importance." As it turns out, actor Jimmy Stewart, my mom's movie idol, sat a few feet away from us on the beach. At the time, we laughed at the comedic chain of events.

She also told me that the spirit of someone who died in a fire came through to her. I did have a cousin whose son died in a fire as a two-year-old baby. He loosened the cap on a gasoline container in their back yard. The container burst into flames, and the young boy died. But the interesting part of Janet's reference to this person is that it also connects to an event involving my daughter when she was a teenager. Cameron was standing with a girlfriend on a street corner in Montreal, Canada, near McDonalds. A car with a group of young men drove up—a couple jumped out and tried to pull her into the car. Then all of a sudden, for no apparent reason, they looked startled, let her go, jumped in their car, and raced away. She looked up to see a young man, with burn scars on his face, who had appeared by her side. Still shaky, she and her girlfriend went into McDonalds. Once inside, the young man with the scarred face came to her and asked if she was all right. She said "yes," and he walked toward the door. Suddenly, she had an urge to run after him. She got to the door just as he exited, but no one was there! He had disappeared. She said she knew that she had just met her guardian angel. So when Janet asked whether I knew anyone who had died in a fire, I felt she was picking up the same person who had helped my daughter so many years ago.

The specificity of many of Janet's remarks has been most impressive to me. For example, she told me that my daughter had been recently involved with two individuals whose first names began with "Jo" and "Mo". The names were Jocelyn and Monika. In 2008, she told me I would soon be attending a "unique wedding." That summer I attended a same-sex marriage. On another occasion, she told me that we were having work done with the siding on one side of the house, and she identified the exact location. After looking at the images on Google Earth, taken a couple of years earlier, I saw that she could not have seen that we had removed the siding on an outside wall in order to change a window. Construction was ongoing at the time of our talk. In an earlier reading, she told me that I had a major water leak; and two years later, we had to drill a second well because of ongoing water problems. (We were having problems at the time of the reading, but I didn't attach significance to the idea of a leak—and I still don't know whether the problems originated in whole or part from a leak. However, we definitely had a water problem for many years, causing major trauma when we ran out of water on the day of my daughter's Alexandra's wedding, when relatives visited, and every major holiday occasion.)

Finally, I have been impressed by the way that the messages reflect the personalities of the individuals with whom Janet connects. For example, my mother often used the term "doozy," and Janet used this term when conveying a message from my mother. Another time, she conveyed a message from a deceased friend who said that I was his "cross to bear in this life." These were the very same words that he used so many times when speaking of our relationship.

I could mention many other points that validate the readings I have received from Janet; however, I have omitted some of the more dramatic points because they are too personal to include.

I didn't know they were on the other side!

As a research scientist I don't know how to explain mediumship and I've been a disbeliever for most of my life, until I had a reading from Janet in December 2009. The first person who came through was my friend and fellow scientist Warren, who is a generation older than me and retired. Janet described him as a "father figure" for me, gave some details about him, and said he passed away of a disease. There was no doubt from Janet's detailed description that she was talking about my longtime friend Warren, but I was confused, because he and I keep in touch and I thought he was still living in Oregon. I called Warren the next day to say hello, feeling confident that he was still alive, and his wife answered the phone and told me that he'd died a few months earlier of a disease. She had wanted to let me know about his death just after it occurred, but she couldn't find my phone or email information among his files.

The second person who came through in Janet's reading was my cousin Vince, whom I'd grown up with. Janet identified him as my cousin and said that he had a Ph.D. He is the only member of my extended family who has a doctoral degree. Once again, I didn't accept this information, because for sure the family would have contacted me if Vince had died. I decided to look him up on the Internet and found his obituary; he'd died just a month earlier. Once again, his family had trouble finding any contact information for me.

In retrospect, it was fortunate that the families of my two dead friends didn't know how to contact me. The fact that I didn't know about these two deaths means that Janet could not have been reading my mind, because I had no knowledge of their passing, but instead she was in touch with another realm where this information was available to her (but not to me!).

I first learned about Janet and her abilities from reading Dr. Gary Schwartz's book "Medium." I was pleased, as a scientist, that she and a few other mediums had had their mediumistic abilities authenticated in double-, triple- and quadruple-blind scientific studies conducted by Dr. Schwartz. I first contacted Janet from a new Yahoo email account I never used again, so that she would have no concrete information about me. She knew only my first name and my unlisted phone number. I paid her with an anonymous postal money order and mailed it in an envelope with a fake return address—I was never going to see that money order again! I did not tell her one word about why I wanted a reading from her. As incredible as it seems, based upon knowing nothing about me but my first name and phone number, Janet somehow knew that my colleague and my cousin had passed on.

Later in the reading Janet correctly identified my wife, Karen, who had passed away from cancer less than a year before. Janet described some of my wife's characteristics that were specific just to her and would not apply to anyone else. Janet also knew that I was involved in a situation related to insurance—which was true, since I was in the process of having to change my health insurance carrier for the first time in 14 years. Janet also knew the obscure and unfindable (even on the Internet) fact that my father was a commercial fisherman.

I can imagine that Janet could know about my insurance situation or my family history by means of telepathy—plucking facts out of my mind in some inexplicable way—that alone would be a wondrous power for her to have! However, I can't begin to imagine how she knew that my cousin and my colleague were dead when I was not privy to this information. The fact that Janet knew about these two deaths when I did not is all the proof I need to believe in an afterlife that Janet is somehow in touch with.

Famous Folks

When Carol and Roland decided to have a reading with me they made a number of choices to keep me in the dark, so to speak. First, they each had their reading a year apart. Besides that, they used different last names, didn't mention each other's name in their own reading, used different phone numbers and were in different states at the time of the call. Carol called from their home in Pennsylvania and Roland called a year later from their summer home in Maine. It's obvious that you'll see it didn't matter if one called from Mars and the other from Jupiter. Spirit has a way of connecting the dots no matter where you are. Carol and Roland chose to combine a number of unique validations from their readings. Some of the information matched, meaning I shared the same thing to them about a loved one, whereas some of the information I gave to each was quite different.

Carol's reading had a lot of twists and turns, like most of my readings—I give what I get and then move to the next thing. Jack, Carol's brother, "The laughing man" as I dubbed him, came through and I described him as Jack or John who passed from cancer. He was Jack and he did pass from cancer. He was a scientist who didn't believe in anything that couldn't be scientifically proven. So, when he showed up, the vision I saw was of him pointing to a picture of Einstein and laughing, as if to say, "See how dumb it was not to believe in anything I couldn't see or prove." Carol smiled since he used to make fun of her all the time because she believed in the afterlife and he didn't. He further identified himself by pointing to an anchor on his cap. Carol informed me that he was a serious boater who built a working quarter-scale tugboat by himself and sailed it around the lake where they have a summer home.

The next thing mentioned was the fresh clean outdoor smell, followed by the image of a log cabin "out in the sticks." Running water nearby and a strong attachment to the land—the log cabin needed repair as well. Carol informed me she is the third generation to own that island, in a large lake in Maine. Sitting on it is a log cabin which was purchased in 1926 by her grandfather. He bought the land because he wanted a remote location to write what became the Pulitzer Prize winning biography of Walt Whitman. The land has been in the family ever since, being passed down from generation to generation. At the time of the reading Carol's husband was working on a major project, the log cabin. He was enclosing the porch to make an additional bedroom and bathroom. During the reading I saw wood being chopped and Carol informed me her husband had chopped wood for the fireplace earlier that day.

Carol also had a number of famous people drop in on us. One, a Hollywood star and the other, a famous political type figure. It doesn't happen often that I receive one famous spirit, let alone two. Carol offered to share a personal story that emerged after her reading.

Dear Janet,
I would like to tell you a story about events that have happened

to me since my reading with you last September. This is a long letter because I feel the need to explain this to you. It is a wonderful story, so please bear with me.

I once told you in an e-mail after my reading that I felt I was receiving "word" communications from a deceased famous relative whom I had become interested in about ten years ago; when I discovered that he and I are related. These communications started after my September phone reading with you in which he came through clearly as part of one of the two groups of "famous" people in my family tree that you connected with. The group was "Hollywood film." His name was (is) Richard Boone, and he is from the generation preceding mine. He and I are directly descended from Daniel Boone's parents: me from Daniel and Richard from Daniel's brother Squire.

Richard died in 1981, and his main occupation was as an actor, but he was also a painter. Since becoming interested in him, I have seen quite a few of his films and TV performances and have come to be a real fan of his work. I also felt "strangely connected" to him - I can't explain it, but that's the best way I can put it.

Well, the "word" communications were all clear connections to my favorite performances by him, and they were not normal, everyday words. They came in books I was reading, music (a song about an outlaw he played in an old Western), cassette tapes, old films, and current TV programs. There were about 15 words that came through to me as obvious communications.

You advised me to thank him and ask him for a feeling to go along with a communication—ask him to give me more.

Well, he did—in spades! He devised a way that was so ingenious that when I realized what had happened and realized that it could only be him, I started to cry and almost couldn't stop. It went back to something that I truly loved in my childhood that has come back into my life 50 years later: one day about two weeks after I thanked Richard and asked him for more, I suddenly remembered a musical album that I so loved as a child. I felt strangely compelled to find the album on Amazon.com. I remembered two specific songs that I loved, and I longed to hear them again—after 50 YEARS! The album was still available, and I ordered it.

When the album came, and I was listening to one of my

two favorite songs, suddenly I started to cry and was filled with a feeling of unconditional love (I was at the gym on the treadmill, and I felt somewhat foolish!). It hit me so hard! And there was an unmistakable connection between the artist on this album of 50 years ago (Danny Kaye) and Richard Boone, having to do with show business and a specific awards show. There is NO WAY this was a coincidence. I also realized that I would have totally missed this if I had not been open to receiving more communication from him. I was open—thanks to you.

I was thrilled, and I thanked him profusely. I never met him in our earthly life, but for some reason there is a strong connection between us, and he chose to get through to me. This happened in April, 2008.

The most amazing part of this story is yet to come. One day at the end of May, I felt compelled—pushed—to sit down at the computer. I don't really like the computer, and I only go on it briefly, usually to check my e-mail and to order things occasionally. I had no idea what I was going to do, but I ended up searching a Richard Boone web site from which I have ordered films of his and articles of interest about his life.

I was not on this site for two minutes when I came upon a painting by Richard that I recognized because a picture of it had appeared in a 2000 biography of his life that I had read. He had painted it in early 1959 when he was on Broadway in New York portraying Abraham Lincoln (also a distant relative of mine). The painting was entitled "Peter and the City" and was signed. It was inspired by his six-year-old son Peter—it was a view of the City at night, as seen by a six-year-old child. It was a magical painting—part of the night sky looked like pink cotton candy, and one of the buildings looked like it was covered in gum drops! When the painting was completed, Richard's son Peter was so excited about it that Richard started to paint again on a regular basis. Richard said that the fact that he was a big western star on TV (Paladin, *of Have Gun Will Travel*) didn't impress Peter half as much as this painting did! Richard had not painted since before WWII.

Richard's wife was so taken with the painting that she did not want him to give it to UNICEF, the charity organization that had asked famous people to contribute art works so the charity could auction them off. He did end up giving it to UNICEF. Someone bought it, and over the years she wondered where it was.

Without even thinking and not knowing why, I bid on the painting. It was offered on a three-day auction only on E-bay, and I came upon it the first day it was offered. I just kept bidding on it—I HAD to have that painting!!! At the end of the auction, I was the winner. Why I had bid on it was a mystery to me—it was certainly more money than I wanted to spend, and I have never bought any art on the internet. The painting was not something that meant anything to me.

When it was delivered to my home on June 7, 2008, I opened the package and looked at the painting, and I was captivated. I was so happy I had it that I immediately started to think about where in my home I would hang it. As I looked at it, I had a very strong thought in my mind that I couldn't hang it, because I didn't own it! A voice in my head said that the painting belonged to Peter Boone, Richard's son. It really had always belonged to him, in the truest sense, because he had inspired it.

Then I had the thought to contact the author of the Richard Boone biography, ask him to contact Peter Boone, and tell him that the painting had surfaced, and that I wanted to give it to him. It seemed so right to do this.

As soon as I made this decision, I immediately felt the sensation of someone slapping me on the back saying, "Good job! I'm proud of you!" This feeling was VERY strong.

On June 9, 2008, I wrote to the book's author, and on June 18 Peter Boone called me—he was thrilled at the possibility of getting the painting. When he told his mother, she was so excited she cried and told him that she had been having dreams about the painting! It means so much to her (she is 87 years old and in poor health). The day Peter called me, June 18, was his father's birthday, he told me. Coincidence? I don't think so.

So, I sent the painting to Peter. He wrote everything down while I told him about the sequence of events that occurred leading me to send the painting to him. He has attached that and his and his mother's thoughts and remembrances to the back of the painting so that his children, grandchildren, etc. will always have the wonderful story behind the painting.

Peter thanked me profusely, and his mother called me and

wrote to me. She was very emotional about it—she is overjoyed that Peter now has this magical painting that he had loved so much as a child—just as I have those songs that I had loved so much as a child and had not heard in 50 years. Going back 50 years to our childhoods, Peter and I have been blessed. The obvious connections to our childhoods and something very much loved is unmistakable. I know that these connections were "orchestrated" by a spirit by the name of Richard Boone.

Janet, because of the very improbable sequence of events that has happened, I can't help but think that I have been a part of a wonderful, spiritual thing—someone in spirit form working with someone in human form to accomplish something very important to one of them (and now both of them). I feel transformed and have lost all fear of death. I feel very grateful and honored that I was trusted with this task. When I heard the joy in Peter's voice and heard that his mom had been dreaming about the painting, I felt humbled beyond measure.

What a wonderful Universe! I owe you thanks, too. If you had not been so very accurate during my reading and so nice to me answering my questions, I doubt if I would have been so open to Spirit contacting me.

I can't begin to tell you how grateful and wonderful I feel. Still amazed on one level, but a true, true believer that we do not cease to exist when we depart our physical body. What an adventure!

God bless you for using your gift for the good of people here on earth and also, I have learned, for the souls in spirit form. I am sure that Richard Boone thanks you too.

Blessings to you, and thank you again.

Carol

Roland, Carol's husband had his reading a year after hers. As he writes:

"I've mentioned some of the highlights from my reading, the really unexplainable ones which could not have been known to you by any amount of research, even if you knew who I was and my background, which you did not. I even disguised myself from you any connection with Carol by using a different phone number in a different state."

While working on Roland's reading I was shown "the land in the woods on the lake" and "the laughing man." I knew I had seen them before and that there was some type of a connection to Carol's reading the previous year. I was very excited the Spirits were re-connecting.

This reading for Roland began with Charles Bronson. Crazy as it seems, while working on Roland's reading, Charles Bronson's face was following me around for days. You may laugh when I say, "I saw his face in the bush outside my office window," but it's true. I even took a picture of it. A couple days later, I was in a pizza parlor and Charles Bronson's face was taped on the window where you watch the worker tossing the dough in the air. The fact this pizza place was 120 miles from my home should be noted as well. So when I began talking about Charles Bronson, Roland was at a loss for words. It made no sense to him, so he said he would ask his wife about it when he got off the phone. It wasn't until after the reading and weeks later I received a response. Carol felt this was her relative Richard Boone playing a practical joke on us. She informed me that he was noted for his practical jokes. Richard was also a big help to Charles Bronson's career in the beginning according to Carol. Richard helped him get parts in two of his series, *"Medic"* and *"Have Gun Will Travel."* This was a good way for him to get exposure for his budding career. I was glad to find out about the connection and interestingly enough after Roland's reading, Charles Bronson no longer appeared to me. Remember, I didn't even know who Roland was, so I couldn't connect him to Richard Boone.

Roland commented that one very interesting thing I was being shown was a microwave oven flying around. At first I couldn't understand why I was seeing this, then I asked the obvious question, even if it seemed somewhat crazy: Did a man you know invent the microwave? Roland enthusiastically said, "Yes!" I was speechless and then laughed, asking "Really?" At this time I also mentioned a problem with a patent. Roland explained: This wasn't completely accurate, as Charles Townes (Carol's first cousin twice removed) didn't invent the microwave, but he used that technology to invent the Maser and then he built on that technology to invent the Laser (Light Amplification by Stimulated Emission of Radiation.), for which he received the Nobel Prize in Physics in 1964. You mentioned a fight over a patent. I wasn't aware of it at the time, but after reading Charles Townes' book on how the laser came to be invented, I found out that he went to a number of legal proceedings in defense of the patents for the laser, which were held by his employer, Bell Labs, and for which he was handsomely rewarded. They won all the legal cases, which established him as the first person to postulate the theory of the laser.

155

I also was given the vision of the Underground Railroad. Visions of the secretiveness, fleeing your home, running, and hiding out, fear for your life, were impressed upon me. Since this has come through in only a handful of readings in the past and they all were spot on, I knew this was going to fit for him as well. So at first Roland wondered how it could possibly relate. He explained he was an immigrant who came to the U.S. with his family as a young boy. No one in his European family was in America at the time prior to 1949, so there couldn't have possibly been any kind of connection. When we talked about it at some length, it finally dawned on Roland what I was seeing: a similar experience that his family lived through during the Second World War. As he describes:

We were indigenous German people living in eastern Czechoslovakia. When I was a little over a year old and my mother was literally nine months pregnant, we were forced to become refugees, leaving our home and all our possessions behind as we were fleeing the advancing Russians and the Slovak partisans who were taking away or killing our German-speaking neighbors whose only crime was that they were Hitler's excuse for taking over the country. My family saw them marching our neighbors away at gunpoint, never to be seen again. On our way to Germany, a distance of several hundred miles, we had to hide in the woods, in trenches, culverts and under bridges. We had bombs dropped on our train, we were shot at and attacked. I guess what you saw was in the context of what you had previously seen and understood.

I was thankful that Roland shared this story so it can show you how I received pieces of my information. Mediumship is not an exact science, yet seeing something that relates to an emotion can reveal a parallel situation. Because of the way I receive information, I think the feeling from a loved one on the other side shows me a scene I could personally relate to. Each medium has their own personal library of information from personal experiences. Years ago I was in a home that was used as part of the Underground Railroad and I saw an actual tunnel in which many slaves supposedly traveled. When I now get a vision like this from the other side, I know what it means. Because I couldn't begin to understand Roland's experience, I believe I was shown the tunnels and fear and running to connect the two.

Roland also wrote:

Also, out of the blue you mentioned David Bloom. He was the NBC weekend host of the Today show who died from Deep Vein Thrombosis during his stint in Iraq. You mentioned you saw ahead of time that he was going to die, but there was nothing that you could do about it. It turns out he died of the same cause as my father. A blood clot in his leg cut loose, went to his lungs and killed him. You didn't know why you were seeing this, but I knew right away this was correlating with my father's similar death.

You also saw a problem on my forehead and I subsequently went to the surgeon a few months later to remove a pre-cancerous lesion which was exactly where you saw it. If it hadn't been for your warning, I wouldn't have done anything about it, since it looked so inconsequential being about the width of a pencil eraser and mostly hidden by my hairline.

I have to say that much of your readings and subsequent follow-up let us know that you are the real deal. You have given us such peace of mind and now we do not fear the unknown and unknowable that comes after this earthly life. Thanks so much for your helpful insights and your kind reassurances.

All our love,
Roland and Carol

Chapter Ten

Our Children Who See

Don't limit a child to your own learning, for he was born in another time.
Rabbinical saying

The children's chapter was originally going to include only stories from the other side, until my son, Matt, reminded me of many of his personal experiences, some that I have personally played a part in. So instead, I'll recount a number of our stories first, then share a few stories from clients. Hopefully, if your son or daughter has experienced anything similar, Matt's stories will help the skeptic within you to be more open in the future. Allowing your children's psychic senses to bloom with support and love can bring them a sense of peace about their future.

Michael & Matt

At age two-and-a-half, a young boy from Oklahoma named Michael was sitting on the couch with his dad when he randomly said, "I used to be a train engineer, I used to drive trains." His dad, Big Mike, was taken aback over this bit of news from out of the blue. As he recalls, there was no television on, they didn't have any books on trains, and Michael was so matter of fact about it that Big Mike simply did not know what to say, so he acknowledged Michael's story in a blasé manner. Time moved on and Michael began to remark about components and functioning parts of trains in normal conversation. He even mentioned types of trains and the characteristics of the particular trains. Since his parents knew little to nothing about trains, they were intrigued by his remarkable knowledge. His Mom, Lori, decided to investigate. She drove to the local library hoping to discover information about the trains Michael mentioned. She also wanted to see if he was making it up, or if particular trains really did exist. What she found amazed her: Michael actually knew what he was talking about. On top of that, he knew about older trains that no longer existed, which surprised her even more. Considering that Michael has never been exposed to trains in *any way* this story becomes even more phenomenal. Lori had to admit he did seem to have a special connection to them. When Lori called to relay her story, I listened, then had one of my own to share.

I began by explaining when my son, Matt, was one-and-a-half, he loved when I read to him, and we sat for hours as I read book after book. One morning while reading to him he looked up at me and said, "Mom, I like you much better than my other parents in Florida. They never used to read to me." Like Michael's dad, I just said the first thing that I could muster up after such a comment, "Well thank you honey, I'm glad you like us better." I remember giving him a one-arm hug, while holding the book thinking, *Wow, where did that come from?* We had never been to Florida with Matt and we live in Missouri, far from Florida. I went on to explain to Lori that I began to buy him Florida-related items such as ocean-fish cards, books and even a map. Whenever I added those items in the mix, he always gravitated toward them. When he was about ten we went to Florida and he made a comment I'll never forget. He said, "Mom, I feel different when being here. Like I've been here before." Well, I know for a fact Matt had never been to Florida previously, at least in this life. I've come to accept and believe through my readings and personal experiences that we continue to exist once we leave our body here. I also believe that we will be, or can be, reincarnated. Lori and I both agreed it was possible that Michael and Matt shared a little of the wisdom that they remembered from a previous life when they came back this time around.

I believe that children have a natural connection to the other side since they haven't yet been influenced by many of our society's close-minded teachings. Their natural sense of self allows them to be open to whatever they sense or see. If your child expresses such comments, try to make it a positive experience, but also try not to be gullible either. I didn't badger my son with questions after he made that comment about his "previous parents" not reading to him, I just acknowledged it. As with "crazy talk" or "make believe" you might just shut off whatever natural connection to a past life they may still hold. If nothing else, write down in a journal each time they mention something, whether six months or six years later (or maybe never again). That way you will have a reminder of your child's undefiled comments—if nothing else, it will make for a good topic of discussion when they get older.

***

Many months after Matt's "Florida parents" story, I was amazed by a statement he made one afternoon. He was no more than two years old when I was trying to put him down for a nap. It was New Year's Eve and we were planning on being out late. Hoping Matt would fall in with my plans, I laid him down—he was not accommodating. Instead, he cried and fussed as I stood out of sight around the corner. Suddenly, he began screaming at the top of his lungs. The sound was so deafening, I quickly ran in, thinking he may have hurt himself in the crib. As I got to his side, he was standing and pointing to the far corner. Eyes wide, he was yelling, "That man, that man, told me to take a nap." With chills down my spine, I slowly turned around to see an empty corner. Matt was seeing something I couldn't. I picked him up and held him, telling him, "It's okay honey, he's not going to hurt you, he's trying to help Mommy." Matt continued to cry, and so I decided he didn't need a nap after all, he was up till 1:30 the next morning without taking a nap.

When Matt was old enough I nonchalantly asked him one day if he remembered the man in the corner of his bedroom and he thought about it for a minute and said, "I do remember, but vaguely. I saw a tall figure of a man. He looked translucent and colorful like what things look like after glancing at the sun." Matt's violent screams must have frightened this man away, for Matt never saw him again.

***

Standing in the bedroom, wrapping paper in hand, I realized I needed scissors to wrap a birthday present for the party that night. Carl began to discuss the evening plans, when Matt walked in the doorway. He said, "Here Mom," as he walked towards me carrying the scissors.

I looked at him surprisingly and asked, "What is this for?"

In a matter of fact manner he replied, "You said you wanted the scissors."

Thinking to myself, yes I wanted the scissors, but no I never verbally asked for them, I responded, "What made you bring the scissors to me?"

"I don't know, I just heard you say you needed the scissors somehow in my head and since I was in the kitchen I got the scissors out of the drawer and brought them in to you," he answered.

"Well, thank you honey, that was very nice of you," I said as I took the scissors from his hand and gave him a kiss on the cheek.

When he walked out of the room, Carl looked at me and said, "That was freaky!"

I shook my head and said, "Actually, it was kind of cool. I just wish he would have brought the tape too!"

This was clearly a sign of mental telepathy. What I found so fascinating was the fact that Matt was in the kitchen, knew where the scissors were located and brought them to me without really thinking much about it. I didn't make a big deal out of it except for asking a couple of curious questions, then let it go. By accepting it as a normal happening, I felt it would encourage Matt to continue using telepathy in daily life.

***

As Matt came home from high school one afternoon, he told me he heard a voice in his head telling him something was going to happen and he wanted to tell me about it.

"Mom, what I heard wasn't really anything of major importance, but I should have listened."

Intrigued, I asked, "Okay, so what did you hear?"

"Well," he said slowly, "When I walked into the classroom, I heard a voice in my head say, "Don't use your favorite mechanic pencil or you'll lose it." I know that sounds stupid Mom, but that's what I heard. Anyway, I was thinking that it was a stupid thought so I continued to use the pencil."

I could see where this was going and said, "Go on."

"Well, I was being careful with it, I thought, but at the end of the day I realized I lost it. It really ticked me off. Why would a voice tell me something so trivial anyway, how stupid is that?"

I replied, "Well Matt, you should listen to that voice within, because next time it may not be so trivial. Besides, it sounds like that voice within was right, since you did lose it."

"So," I asked, "Why were you so mad?"

"Well because I not only lost an expensive pencil, it is like I made the choice to lose the pencil, I didn't listen!" he said.

Deciding not to mention how I often feel the same way when I think he isn't listening to me, I instead chose the high road and stated, "Well, it's a lesson learned."

"Well, last time was trivial too Mom," Matt said.

"What do you mean last time?" I asked surprisingly.

"Well, the other day I was with Dad at the grocery store and we had your list. As I walked by the frozen food aisle I heard, "Go down that aisle." I stopped, but since nothing was on the list in the frozen foods, we just kept walking. Anyway, we checked out and when I got to the car, it suddenly dawned on Dad, we did need something down that aisle."

"It sounds like someone is trying to help you, Matt."

"But it's trivial stuff, nothing important."

"Like I said before, maybe next time, it won't be so trivial. You need to remember that. Someone on the other side may be trying to make you pay attention in case there does come a time that voice within is going to be useful," I said, "and, keep in mind, they are letting you know that you always make the ultimate decision, they are just being helpful. It's your choice whether to pay attention or not."

Matt doesn't only have daytime intuitiveness—he often has nighttime occurrences, which are so vivid that I believe he is doing more than just dreaming.

While laying in bed, I woke up one morning and saw Matt walk out of his bedroom, cross the hall and walk into the bathroom. I didn't hear the door shut and thought that was odd, but figured he was probably still sleepy and didn't bother. About a minute later my husband, Carl walked in to kiss me goodbye before he left for work and asked if he should wake Matt up for school. I informed him he was already up and in the bathroom. Carl just looked at me strangely and said, "I just walked by his room and he's in bed."

"No, he's not, I saw him walk across the hall to the bathroom," I replied firmly.

"Honey, he's in bed!" Carl argued.

"No he's not, he's in the bathroom!" I argued back.

"Nobody is in the bathroom, Janet. Matt's sleeping."

"OK, well I just saw someone walk by," I said, "and it looked exactly like Matt."

Not believing Carl, I got up to look. Sure enough, he was sleeping. That made me stop and think about what I saw. It was a full body figure of what looked like Matt in some shadows due to the early morning. I could see the texture of his hair and facial features.

Carl left for work and so I went back in to wake Matt up. As he got ready for school he came into the kitchen and said sleepily, "Hey Mom, I had the strangest dream. I felt like I was physically at the lake house."

This prompted me to ask what the dream was about, especially after "seeing him" earlier walk by.

He went on to explain, "I felt like I was at Aunt Sue's and Uncle Glenn's lake house. I was walking to the blue chair by the door and then sat down in it, then realized I had to go to the bathroom so I got up to go—only it was our bathroom. When you woke me up, it took me a couple minutes to realize I wasn't in the bathroom...It was weird..."

I turned slowly with a smile and looked at him with wide eyes. I think my son was astral traveling and I just witnessed it. I had a flashback, remembering as a child seeing my father in the doorway. Well, if my father could do it, I guess my son can too. I'll admit, it left me feeling a little off balance. Knowing I just witnessed my son astral traveling through the house was a little eerie. On the other hand, it reiterated my belief that we don't need our bodies to exist. I always have that visual of unzipping ourselves out of the "body suit" when we die. I guess we don't have to wait until death to unzip after all! Too early for such a lesson, I needed my morning coffee.

I would like to add that I have never pressured my son to hold any of my own beliefs. What he gets, he gets on his own. Matt has told me quite specifically that he isn't ready to do more of this work at this time. Although he is quickly gaining more confidence and courage, I leave his spiritual and psychic development up to him. I'm completely fine with that, especially because I know how difficult it was for me. It is his choice and his life, and I respect that, only reminding him to pay attention in case that voice within gives him a warning. One thing he does know and that is I'm here for him if he ever needs me. As a child I never felt I had anyone to talk to about my visions and so I was often too frightened to talk about them, allowing those visions to build until I became panicked about what I would see next. I also constantly thought no one would understand or believe me. I never gave my parents the chance to even try to help. So I ask that you, the parent, allow yourself to be open to any comments your children may share about their own psychic experiences, large or small. Simply taking note of what they are saying will comfort them. This will teach them to embrace life to a greater capacity, far beyond what society would have you first imagine.

***

While laying the foundation for this chapter, the other side presented me with a situation to write about that I couldn't afford to pass up.

After attending my son's racquetball game after school one evening, I left the fitness club where it was held and headed home. Matt drove separately since he was coming from school with his cousin, Tyler, another member of the team. He had to drop Tyler off at his car in the school parking lot and then he would be following shortly behind. By this time it was around 5:30 and rush hour traffic was now bumper to bumper on Interstate 270. I was listening to music on the radio when suddenly my *languages* began to come through strongly. The abrupt tone made my adrenaline race and energy fly down my arms to my fingertips as they grasped the steering wheel. Although I do not understand the specific words as the language forcefully emerges, I can tell by the pressure it exerts in my throat and off my tongue that the energy was striking a familiar warning. I knew immediately that something important was happening at this moment. A quick mental flash brought me back to a recent trip to New York where we met up with some friends on Long Island. While they were showing us the sights, we passed a beautiful home that was previously owned by Billy Joel. I commented on how the song, "Only the Good Die Young" reminded me of my grandma Eleanor. I explained how events took place after she passed and that one specific phrase of the song reminded me what a wonderful person she was and that she died too soon.

A fairly uncommon song in this day and age, "Only the Good Die Young," written and performed by Billy Joel, played at that precise moment on the car stereo. This triggered an immediate red flag, and I knew this warning was directed toward my son, Matt. Months earlier, that phrase played over and over as I walked through the house hearing "Only the Good Die Young." It was then as I walked into my son's room I heard it pop up on his cell phone, his ring tone of choice that week. I just shook my head and smiled. When I asked him about it, he said he had such a great time in New York, including the drive past Billy Joel's previous home. After hearing the story about Billy Joel's song and my grandma he thought it was really cool and wanted that song as a ring tone because it made him feel good as well. That was fine as long as he didn't get any ideas from the song.

So, here I am, stuck in traffic and having this sudden overwhelming feeling hit me. Although I have a rule of not talking on the cell phone in the car if I'm driving, I knew I had to call him and tell him to be careful. As I was reaching for my purse, my phone rang. I grabbed it knowing it was Matt calling. I answered and on the other end Matt's voice was shaky. He had been in a car accident, but was okay. It was a minor crash, but enough to shake up a sixteen-year-old driver.

It is moments like this when it's quite obvious that those on the other side can not only see me, but see those around me and know what is going on in our daily life. My journey has been extremely complicated, because I'm working with languages I don't understand. Impressions from the energy that flows through me, in combination with my other senses help me comprehend it in some form, which in my case led to the correct conclusion. Although I couldn't stop the accident from happening, the language at least gave me a heads-up so I could be calm and rational for my son at a time when he needed me.

Matt is now in college. As an elective and a personal desire, he began painting. He expressed to me one day while chatting on the phone that often when he paints he feels that he is channeling another energy. He'll make brush strokes for no apparent reason only to realize later it's exactly what he needed. They seem to be mistakes at first, but upon closer inspection, it's obvious they belong there. Sharing stories about my son has been a good way to allow you, the reader, to experience how something so simple or even so seemingly meaningless can mean so much. If your child follows their intuition and expresses it in a positive environment, then they and those around them will often find more rewards in life simply by expanding their awareness *to* life.

***

Crash

In August 2009, Christine, whose stories are also shared in Chapter nine, (In my Mind, I'm Goin' to Carolina), generously offered me the opportunity to include another story from her reading as well. I feel this was a perfect way to show you, the reader, that sometimes we have to experience turmoil in order to learn the significance of the future. Such was the case for her son, Brennen:

"Although many validations were given by Janet, three things continue to amaze me even to this day. The first was when she had mentioned that my sixteen-year-old son, Brennen, would be in a "crash." She said that my guides wanted me to know he wouldn't be seriously hurt, but he would have some minor physical injury. She came back to this topic three times in the reading, adding more information each time: The crash would be an accident that occurred at or around school; Brennen would either run into something or something would hit him; it would happen in early November. The third time Janet mentioned the crash, she said that something would result from this accident that would be important for me to follow up with. November rolls around and I get a call at work from Brennen's school. In gym class, another student had accidentally hit Brennen in the eyebrow with a badminton racquet. At the hospital, the doctor was preparing to stitch up the wound when Brennen's heartbeat spiked to over 200 beats per minute; he was in SVT (supraventricular tachycardia), apparently due to a high level of stress and/or fear. They quickly brought his heartbeat down using an IV sedative and completed the stitches. This is a very dangerous condition that temporarily deprives the brain of oxygen. It requires monitoring and quick action (specific breathing techniques) should it happen again."

***

This chapter would not be complete without sharing a couple of stories about the wonderful children who now reside on the other side. A number of my clients were gracious enough to share parts of their reading. Their children have shown us, "You can take the impossible and make it possible." These words were spoken by a young man who showed his Mom as well as myself what true words of wisdom they are.

I'm taking the impossible, and making it possible!

Ryan's Mom states:

About four months after our son was killed, I began looking for a medium. If an existence beyond death was possible, I needed to know that Ryan was "okay."

A friend of a friend recommended a website for the Forever Family Foundation since the mediums listed there have participated in studies that rate their level of accuracy to a certain degree. I felt this might be a good place to start.

Most of the mediums were in another state and at that time I thought I really needed to have my reading "face to face" so that I would be able to believe what I was told. I also worried that Ryan either couldn't be contacted or that he was having a difficult time with the transition. Since Janet was in Missouri, I emailed to request a reading.

Janet's words brought the first moment of peace I'd had since Ryan's death. I will always be grateful to her for the gift she has and her generosity in the way she uses it.

The reading began with:

"Tell Mom she's going to see me on TV again!"

Janet asked, "Is this Ryan?," and heard, "Yes," "and he is smiling."

I am still filled with emotion as I read these words! I thought, "Is this really possible?"

As the reading continued, so did the validations....

Janet stated, "There is a canoe on top of a car.... people are going on a float trip.... the canoe tips over and things are floating away in the current. It is difficult to get back to the canoe which is on the other side...."

The day before Ryan was killed, his dad returned from a "guys" float trip and he was anxious to share the story with Ryan about his adventure. The canoe he was paddling tipped over in the current, and gear floated everywhere. He was banged around on the rocks and stuck on the other side of the river until another boater helped him back to his canoe. (His dad never had the chance to tell his story; Ryan was killed the next morning.)

Ryan was also planning his annual "friends" float trip for about 35 people... which would have been four days after his passing. The list of his friends that were planning to go still sits on his desk.

Janet told me she was being shown cooking references... "pot of water boiling... noodles being put in..." This may have seemed odd to her for a guy his age but was very validating for me. He really liked to cook, especially "healthy" things and one of the best things I remember him making for us was chicken parmesan over linguini. (I credit his cooking skills to the advanced foods class in high school. Not only did they get to eat what they cooked, but the teacher was very attractive as well!)

The next thing Janet told me as a direct quote. "He said he is bringing happiness... Taking the impossible and making it possible." This was a very powerful message for me. It reminds me to consider that perhaps there is more to life, death and everything in between than meets the eye.

A few months before Ryan's passing, he and his sister and I had a conversation in our kitchen about whether or not there really could be something beyond this life since we had lost quite a few family members in recent years, several at a young age. When I expressed that I believed, Ryan replied "I'd like to think that it's possible, but I'm just not sure that it is."

My reading was a few days before Thanksgiving and Janet said she felt a need to get these messages to me before then. She said "He knows you may feel you don't want to give thanks, but do it for him. He gives thanks for all of you." "He is showing me 2-4-6-8-10-12 as if your group for Thanksgiving keeps getting larger."

This was true. Our daughter and her fiancée were planning the meal at their house and what began as a small gathering had turned into a large group.

Janet mentioned that "his sister was making a change, two big changes (giving me the letters ASL with her name, which are correct) since his passing. I'm being shown a mail box... maybe a change of address or mail was delivered to the wrong place..." His sister just became engaged and they purchased a new home the month before.

Janet commented, "I'm smelling the smoke from a pipe... definitely pipe smoke, not cigarette or cigar." "And I have an older man named "Jack."

My grandfather, "Jack," was from Holland and although I only had the opportunity to visit with him during several vacations as a child, his pipe was the one thing I remember most. He entertained us by making sounds with it as though it was a musical instrument... and the smell of pipe smoke is a fond memory for me.

Janet continued, "Ryan said, 'continue with the fun stuff.... parties, float trips, nothing sad. Go to Florida and the water again next year...'"

We have a condo in Florida and have gone there EVERY summer of his life, and the parties.... that really sums up our life "before this" with family and friends.

This next thing is what really convinced me. Janet said, "Was there something about him being turned around wrong at the cemetery? He is kind of laughing about this. He is also showing me that at the funeral it was as if part of the way he is facing one way and the other part he is going another way.... or the others are facing the opposite way."

Ryan's funeral was a firefighter's funeral.... lots of tradition and hundreds, maybe even a thousand or more attending. He was taken to the church and cemetery on a fire truck and was accompanied by his crew. We were not there when the casket was lowered. A week or two after the funeral, his father and I visited the cemetery and the groundskeeper came to speak to us. He said "I just want to let you know that we turned the casket around before we lowered it. There is a regulation at this cemetery that everyone is facing a particular way. We didn't want to make any kind of deal about it the day of the funeral but wanted to make sure you knew that." And as I look through the pictures of the day of his funeral procession.... the stars of the flag on top of the casket are at one end for half of the pictures, and at the other end for the rest of them.

Janet also mentioned that Ryan felt "athletic" (so true!) and that he likes that "you can hear the kids playing" where he is located at the cemetery. This is validating because we picked that spot because you can hear the kids playing baseball at the fields nearby.

The last thing Janet said in our reading..."He feels happy." These three simple words were such a gift. After months of grieving, worrying and wondering....maybe he really is "okay." Although we can never have Ryan back the way we want him, it does help to know that a connection is still there.

Hey!

Scott's Mom Colleen states:

Our driveway, for the first time, was empty of cars and people drove by wondering what was happening inside. In a tragic turn of events, we lost our only son, Scott, at age 27. Just days before, I sat on the floor hiding in my closet trying to catch my breath as the house filled with friends and family that dropped everything to be here, near us. While their intentions were good, visitors could not possibly change the indescribable pain and heartache we were experiencing. We asked to be left alone, giving us space to even begin to comprehend what had just happened, so in silence amazing gifts were left at our door step instead. It was at this time I found the connection back to my son and met Janet Mayer.

In the early mornings, I would cautiously open the front door to get the newspaper and often found gifts of flowers, letters, cards and in this case a very special book that changed the direction of my life. It was left by a dear friend—a life changing book. Crying, as I thumbed through the pages, and wanting more, I took what I remember to be my first breath of comfort and "knowing" the connection between my son and me had not gone away at all, but instead had changed. And so I began a new journey of discovery and knowing with my son.

While reading the book, there were other mediums' names mentioned, but I found myself drawn to Janet, writing her name down several times before actually trying to contact her. On August, 14, 2007, four months since my Scott's passing, I had my first reading with Janet Mayer. There were so many things that had happened in those past months that I couldn't logically explain. I quietly thought I was going crazy but always felt Scott near me, urging me onward as if something was left unfinished. As we began the reading, I was comforted immediately as she described the crinkle on one side in his smile and how he joined us with a hop-step announcing himself with a "Ta-Da!" Unsure of what to expect going into this, it ended with the most peaceful, comfortable feeling of knowing that we were still together. My ten pages of notes were filled with very specific and personal things I felt only Scott and I would have known about. It turned out that this was just the beginning.

On Tuesday, August 28, 2007, Janet sent me a message that she had woke up that morning and had to email me after a reading she had done. The message sent at 8:54am (my time) read, "I'm not really sure why or for what reason, but it was as if Scott came to me and said: Hey, could ya drop my Mom a line today and just say Hey? And so I am… For whatever the reason may be….. Hey! Many Blessings, Janet"

I missed the message that morning as I was headed downtown to pick up a video I had made for Scott's website. On my way home, I was driving in the fast lane about 70 mph, on the freeway when a large farming truck blew out a tire. I heard the explosion and then saw something hit the truck next to me in the middle lane.

It turns out the tire took out the front windshield on the truck beside me, which was hauling a full trailer of stone flooring, and then the tire hit the underside of my truck. It happened very quickly and I wasn't even sure what hit me until we all made it to the side of the road to investigate further. No one was hurt, but we all commented in amazement how lucky we were not to lose control of our vehicles on the freeway.

After exchanging all our information and speaking with the police, I got back in my truck and of course thinking of Scott watching over me; I noticed the time as 8:54am and made a mental note to myself.

It was much later in the day when I arrived home and had a chance to look at messages, at which time I read Janet's message from my son. I immediately replied and thanked her for passing this on. By the way, it was "Hay" not "Hey". The large farming truck I described that blew out a tire was a Flat Bed Hay Semi-Truck.

Colleen's other validations

Cheers

Our son passed on April 7, 2007—in the following months my husband and I would have dinner out at places where Scott had often gone. On the 7th of every month our family dinner date would be at Molly Brannigan's, an Irish pub that Scott had been to after work his last night.

As we placed our order, we studied the room, wondering where he had been standing last or what table was he sitting at. Our drinks would come and while we would look at the empty chairs at our table, we quietly shared between us that Scott is probably sitting right there watching us and thinking we're crazy for being here. We would then raise our glasses and make a toast to Scott on the 7th of every month. This was a very private time for us that only my husband and I knew about.

Four months later in Janet's reading came a message from Scott – "It begins with 'cheers' and toasting to him. He likes that we do this, as it gives him a very happy feeling."

Moved

When Scott was in pre-school my Mom took him shopping for Mother's Day. He came home proud and excited about his very special gift that he picked out himself, just for me. It was a small gold charm in the shape of a happy worm. A perfect gift for a little boy to pick out for his Mom; I wore this for a long time and "worm" even became my nickname at work as co-workers found it endearing. I found the charm again shortly after Scott's passing and placed it in a very specific place that no one but me would know about nor understand. Each day I would look at the little worm and smile, asking Scott to please show me a sign that he can still hear me. With so many odd things happening around us already, I was very comforted and excited to share with my husband that this little worm I had secretly placed, had somehow moved, giving me the sign from Scott I was asking for.

In Janet's reading, a message came from Scott – "Something small moved in the house, something you already know about."

I'm Right Here

A couple of days before Scott's service, the funeral home contacted us for a viewing of our son. My husband and I along with Scott's best friend, Travis, made our way into the Chapel this one last time. It's difficult to explain the feeling of such an event but after standing over him for some time, I sat in one of the pews and could hear him say "I'm right here Mom, that's just the body, I'm right here with you."

I didn't share that story with anyone—I called Travis to share the messages from my reading, and without hesitation he quickly said, "I know where this happened, he was sitting next to you in the Chapel at the viewing, I heard Scott say to you 'I'm right here.' I could feel him there."

In Janet's reading, one message from Scott was, "He's showing me a bench or a place where more than one person can sit. Sometime before or after the service, I was sitting there and Scott was sitting there with me."

Happy Birthday

Its Friday, September 14th, a month after Janet's reading. Scott's Birthday is two days away, on the 16th. Many folks have fallen away from us, still unsure of what to say and do—others remain very close. Scott's friends are part of the close group; Justin lives in Texas and continues to stay in touch, and his parents too, through regular emails and phone calls. The door bell rings and flowers are delivered to me from Justin and his wife Laura—they are beautiful and make me cry and smile knowing the message I had been given earlier.

The message from Scott was, "You will receive something in September, next month. It will be a package, not a card or letter that is from me or related to me."

Not Yet

At the time of the reading some things had already happened, and others would happen in the future. I'm fortunate that I've never broken any bones or seriously been hurt before, so this message put me on alert.

In November 2009, I had been to the doctors several times for my right foot bothering me; it started hurting for no obvious reason. The doctor ran x-rays and referred me to a foot specialist the day before we were scheduled for a very large catering event in Tucson. On the last day of the show, we had sent everyone home early, leaving the two of us to pack up the catering trailers. I stepped backwards and heard my foot crack and then it quickly begin to swell. Unsure to this day what or why it happened, I broke my foot in two places and experienced my first time wearing a cast.

The message from Janet's reading was, "Scott's warning you to be careful of a fall or hurting your foot or ankle."

Many things have changed as I become more confident and aware of the magical signs happening around me every day. Janet and I stay in touch through readings and email as I navigate my way through some of these things that just don't seem possible, but I hold dear to my heart.

These special gifts I share with you come from my heart and my amazing son who gave them to me. I have learned and felt a new meaning to the words "love" and "forgiveness."

Peaceful Hugs and Blessings…Scott's Mom, Colleen.

Chapter Eleven

Our "Other" Children

Until one has loved an animal, a part of one's soul remains unawakened.
Anatole France

Monty

Debbie and her husband Tony's golden retriever, Monty, was very sick, so she asked if I could assist in his healing by the practice of Pranic Healing. Pranic Healing is another important aspect of my life. I was involved in and I attended a number of courses with the distinguished Master Stephen Co. Pranic Healing is an ancient science and art which utilizes Prana or Chi energy to heal the body. It takes on many names and many of you may see this as similar to psychic healing, Reiki or hands-on-healing. I took an advanced course relating to colors and their healing energies. We were taught that this practice can also be used in long-distance healing. This means a body was not required to be in front of us for healing to take place. I was honored to take part in Monty's healing. I headed to my kitchen. I envisioned Monty lying there, on the cool kitchen floor, since that was one of his favorite areas. My healing work began.

I began to sweep him as the course suggested. I could feel his energy—it was heavy and so I focused on sweeping slowly across the entire area of his body. I continued to sweep and sweep, trying to brush away this heavy energy when in my vision, suddenly, I saw him stand up and walk away. Since I never expected this to happen, I sat there wondering, "What exactly did this mean?" Never in my Pranic Healing course had someone walked away from me. Even when sending healing long distance, I had never experienced a vision like this. It was then I realized this wasn't an ordinary healing. Monty was letting me know that it was his time to go. He was leaving, walking into the next world. When I spoke on the phone with Debbie, she stated that he was calm. It seems the tumors had taken over his body—it was his time to move on. I sat on the kitchen floor, and tears just started to roll down my face. I thanked Monty for letting me know. I believe in my heart the Pranic Healing helped him relax that day even though it was time for him to move on. It was only hours later that he passed away.

Several weeks later, Debbie and Tony were in the bedroom. As they were getting ready to grab the ends of the comforter, to uncover the bed for the evening, Debbie froze as she looked down at the end of the bed. What she saw came as a shock. The sudden large impression on the waffled comforter was deep. The outline was obvious. The sudden impression disappeared as a loud familiar thump hit the floor.

Debbie glanced over at Tony asking with wide eyes, "Did you see that?"

To which Tony replied, "Did you hear that?"

Staring at each other, they began to cry. Monty came back in spirit to once again enjoy the comforts they always provided for him and let them know he's still at their bedside, even in spirit.

Tony once commented that Monty often had human-like emotions filter across his face. I personally believe animals have a soul. I've seen visions of dogs, cats, horses, birds, hamsters and even cows. Many times there may just be a face with a floppy ear, or a couple of huge paws appear, but it's their way of letting me know they are over there with family. I believe they drop in on us after they pass to bring comfort, just like they did when alive.

So, next time you hear a woof, a meow or a tweet, maybe they are just offering you a little support you may have needed that day.

Sophie

Friends on Long Island, Phran and Bob, generously welcome me into their beautiful home each time I come to visit. Just as with family, I have come to know their precious cats: Maya, Roswell, Popeye, Olive and Spot, each unique with their own personality. Maya is the furry cat who stays in my room. Actually, it's the other way around, I stay in Maya's room. I'm used to Maya, so it was on the first night of this visit that I was to encounter an unexpected visitor.

The bed is located next to the window and I like to have the blinds pulled open a bit to gaze out at the beautiful trees glistening against the night sky. Climbing into bed, I pulled the covers up and got comfortable. Within moments my buddy Maya jumped up by my feet and walked the path along the side of my body. She completed her journey near the top edge of my pillow and sat in the corner of the bed as if watching over me.

It was then, a second cat jumped up on the bed and cautiously walked across my calves to the opposite side. From there, she proceeded to walk slowly to where my knees were and then she stopped. She sat and just stared at me. I leaned up on my elbow and stared at her thinking at first it was Olive. The more I looked, the more I realized that it wasn't Olive. I wasn't quite sure at this point which cat it was, but one thing I did know was that Maya was the only cat who was supposed to be in my room.

I started to get up and that's when the second cat jumped over my legs and off the bed into the shadowy darkness. I didn't see where she went, so I got up to turn on the light and look for her. I thought I'd better let her out, since this was Maya's room after all. Besides, I was used to Maya, but not this second cat.

I looked around the room and could only see Maya sitting on the corner of my bed staring back at me curiously. I looked under the bed, moved the chair, glanced behind the desk, and saw no other cat. The closet door was cracked open, so I looked in there as well. Since that is where Maya's second bed resides, I figured maybe this second cat was in there hiding. Nothing. I moved pillows, covers, more pillows and still found nothing. I was making so much noise I was waiting for Phran to knock on my door and ask what in the hell was going on. Only silence followed. I sat down on the bed and took a deep breath. I know as clearly as if I was looking at my hand that there were two cats in my room. However, there was no place for the second cat to hide.

I decided I would just go back to bed and this time when the cat jumped up on the bed, I would wait to see where it moseyed off to next. I laid in wait, ready to pounce. I waited so long that I eventually fell asleep. The next morning the sun shone through the big window and I popped awake in bed with a sneaky smile. Now, I'm going to find that second cat and find out which one it is. Looking all over the room, I again saw no other cat besides Maya. I flew through my morning rituals and went downstairs. As I walked in the kitchen there was Phran feeding the cats, all of them, except for Maya. My first thought was, "No way." I proceeded to explain to Phran what happened the night before and apologized for making any noise while searching. That's when she began to question me on what the cat looked like. I explained that at first I thought it was Olive, but immediately knew that was wrong, since the cat was fuller or thicker than Olive. She did have a dark coat, that much I knew. That's when Phran shared the story of Sophie.

Sophie, was their son Jon's cat. As a kitten, she showed up in their yard in the middle of the winter—it was Jon at age three who noticed the little black dot in the deep snow. No matter what the family did, the kitten was too scared to come close. So Jon and Phran set up a shelter for her inside the screened porch and left food for her. This went on for two years until she finally came into the house and joined their other cats. Once she became a member of the house, she somehow managed to keep score and sleep in a different kid's bed each night. So she was never anyone's cat until they moved to the house where they currently reside. By that time she was an older cat and didn't care much for being outside. Her favorite place became Jon's room, where she used to stay even while he was away at college. She considered it her personal room, along with Jon's other menagerie of pets such as gerbils, lizards and birds that inhabited his room. Sophie stayed there even when the door was open and she could roam the house. However, as Sophie prepared to die she would go into the room I was currently occupying. Phran said she had to keep picking Sophie up and bringing her back into Jon's room that night. I think this was Sophie's way of not wanting to leave Jon with her body once she moved on.

After I heard Phran's story, I realized that I'd experienced a family cat, Sophie, manifest physically from the spirit realm. It was a pretty awesome experience and I couldn't wait to see her again. I looked for her that evening and even waited up hoping to see her again. I guess she assumed I would go hunting her down and it wasn't worth the effort. Then again, I wonder if she stopped by my room this time specifically after hearing about the last time I was visiting. We still all laugh about that cat "incident." We'll leave that story for another time.

It was a blessing and honor to have such a wonderful experience of Sophie visiting me.

Thunder

With hurricane Rita approaching the Gulf Coast, Dianne and her family were given a mandatory evacuation notice to "Get out of Dodge" and fast. They were hopeful they would only be gone a day or two, especially since her daughter's cat, Thunder, had accidentally slipped outside and they couldn't find him before leaving.

According to meteorologists' projections, the eye of the storm was to land near their city, but Rita hadn't decided where to land yet. Meanwhile, the family was trapped in traffic that was so backed up, it took them more than twelve hours to reach Huntsville, only 90 miles north of their town.

Fortunately, Rita veered off course and evacuees were allowed to return home. As Dianne's family rounded the corner, they were relieved to see their home intact, although tree limbs and leaves were scattered across the property. They felt sure they had weathered the storm, until they walked inside and realized Thunder was still missing. He had always been an inside cat so they were tremendously concerned.

Here is the email Dianne sent me:

Do you remember the television series, *I Spy* with Bill Cosby? It aired during the 60's or 70's? You may have been too young to remember. Each episode began with a voice recording that said, "I have a task for you, Agent (???), should you decide to accept it."

Here's the deal: On his death-bed, a hospice patient (the one I wrote about in *Afterlife Encounters*—the World War II veteran) gave me his cat to give to my son-in-law. Thunder somehow got out and no one can find him. He's never been outside before—in fact, he's afraid of the outdoors. He's solid black and very sleek. We have searched everywhere we can think of and he's nowhere in sight. My daughter and family live by a forest and bayou. They are very, very upset.

Can you get any sense of where Thunder can be? Any sense that he's dead or alive? Anything at all?

Love, Dianne

I had an appointment that day and didn't get a chance to read her email until late afternoon. I was hopeful that they had already found Thunder but I thought I would see if I could get anything. After I sat down, I tried to envision Thunder and where he might be. I also asked him if he was still here or on the other side? The first thing I saw was him hiding. I saw an enclosed covered area. He seemed alive to me and I felt he was near the house.

I emailed Dianne:

I hope you found your cat. Could Thunder be afraid and hiding in the house or near the house somewhere? I can't picture it exactly, but I keep seeing him in and around the house so I thought I would throw that out there…Hope you find him.

Blessings,

Janet

I also called Dianne and told her I felt that Thunder was alive.

I received an email from her:

Janet, I'm so pleased….AGAIN YOU WERE RIGHT ON. How do you do that? Thunder came home!

My daughter's husband is afraid of psychic stuff, and she has always taken on the beliefs of the men in her life. So when I told her that you said, "I feel he's around, close to home, but hiding. It seems like a dog chased him into something or scared him, and now he's just waiting to get out…… (pause). Yeah, he's around their place, somewhere, and he'll show up after a few days or maybe longer." My daughter said, "She just wants to make us feel better." I let it go.

Well, she called me late last night. They heard meowing at the door, opened it, and there was their cat, thin but unharmed! She immediately called me and asked me to tell you that you are right. She said, "Maybe there's something to your psychic stuff after all."

You never cease to amaze me. Now I'll tell you … My daughter lives on acreage out in the woods and a forest surrounds them. No neighbors close by. I went out to help them search and a huge owl kept screeching and circling overhead. They said, "He ate Thunder." It didn't look good to me either, and I had to wonder if that was the case. It seemed likely.

I've been miserable because my body is covered with chiggers from searching through the woods. Just yesterday I said, "It would have been worth it IF we could have found him," but I had faith in you all along. Your words stayed with me and I believed you, even though I saw the owl.

I'll admit, my rational mind agreed with them—since the owl was so upset that we were in his territory. But in my heart, I believed you.

I can't speak for your accuracy with other people, but I know you've been amazingly accurate with me. Thank you Janet. God bless you.

Love, Dianne

Wanting to understand what I saw in my vision, I called Dianne to ask what the unusual enclosed covered area was, since it didn't seem familiar. I explained that when I sat down to meditate and envisioned Thunder, the first thing I saw was him hiding, then an enclosed covered area, and then I sensed he was alive, near the house. At that point, Dianne informed me that her daughter's home was inside a large airplane hangar. Furthermore, she said that during the months after Rita, Thunder kept dashing outside of the house to hide in different places inside the hangar. Now I understand why, during my vision, I saw an enclosed covered area and felt he was near and around their house.

Buddy

Days before I was to give a reading to a client, I had an interesting vision come through. While closing my eyes, I began to see the name that vaguely looked like "Callie." This prompted me to think "cat" since my brother, his wife and girls have a cat named "Callie." However, I didn't see a cat, and I knew by the energy that was coming through it wasn't a person, so I was confused, but let it go and wrote it down. When I sat down to meditate for a second time for the same upcoming reading, I again got the name "Callie," but this time I heard what sounded *like* Callie. As if stuck on repeat, I kept hearing that word over and over. Then it hit me, this wasn't Callie, it was COLLIE. It was the client's dog, not a cat. I wasn't seeing a name for a cat, but the breed of the dog. Since my abilities come in a variety of forms, I was hearing a name, but not seeing the actual dog. That's not to say the dog was talking to me, but someone was clueing me in from the other side. I had to smile. That was complicated for being such a simple name. The reading took place and I explained the process of how I came about knowing she had a dog, and I thought it was a collie. At the end of the reading the client shared how it was wonderful to hear from her dog, Buddy. He was in fact a collie/husky mix who she had been blessed with for 16 wonderful years. She even admits that at times, she can still hear the jingling of Buddy's collar as he makes his rounds.

I make no claims of being a pet psychic—I do however often see pets on the other side, especially around loved ones.

Cindy

It was at the end of his reading that Roland mentioned they had a recent passing and could I tell him anything about it. He purposely didn't mention who or what and gave no hints.

I listened and focused, trying to see if anyone else would show up. I was taken aback when the "anyone else" actually appeared. Walking into my vision was a dog, which is not what I was expecting. Hesitating, I described what I saw with one word, "dog."

Choked up, Roland knew the obvious reference was his precious 17-year-old-pup, "Cindy," who had died just a couple of weeks prior to the reading.

Also mentioned was the number "two" and digging in a number of areas.

Roland explained that the two referred to their ambivalence in where they were going to bury her, their home in Pennsylvania or their land in Maine.

Interestingly, a year earlier, I gave Roland's wife Carol a reading. In that reading it was mentioned that a gentleman wanted to tell Carol that he loved Cindy or Cynthia. This was Carol's father, who had a special bond with Cindy; whenever he came around Cindy was always extremely excited to see him. Carol and Roland felt this was his way of telling them that when it was her time to pass, he would be there to greet her and take care of her on the other side. Cindy was 17 at the time of her passing and she had been their baby for the past 14 years. She gave them the most wonderfully unconditional love. They still miss her terribly to this day.

In a following reading for Carol, a year after Roland's reading, I mentioned Cindy playing with a "very tiny dog." Carol and Roland agreed this could only have been "Thimble," her mom's dog that was a Toy Manchester. She was only about four or five pounds, soaking wet.

Maggie Moo

Valerie writes:

There were so many significant things that you told me during my reading that it's hard to pick out just a few, as they all were right on the

money. I would have to say one of the most amazing to me was when you asked if "I had a cow buried in the back yard." This was something HUGE, they were telling you about the *cow* in the back yard and even saying ....
"I want to be buried with my cow."

To this day I shake my head in amazement about this, because I *do* have a cow in my back yard. However, it's not really a cow, but my beloved Yorkshire Terrier whose name was Maggie Moo, and years ago a dear friend started calling her "Moo Cow," because of her big brown eyes and her floppy ears. Her nickname stuck and she was always called "Moo Cow." I used to say all the time to my late father-in-law, "when I die I want to be buried with my cow." My beloved "Moo Cow" is indeed buried in my back yard.

Sept. 26, 2005. My beloved 16 year old "Maggie Moo Cow" passes away. I have never felt such pain and grief. I have had animals all my life but have never bonded with an animal like my Moo Cow. For two days I couldn't get out of bed—on the third day, around 2:00 a.m., I got up to go into the kitchen, just before I stepped into the kitchen, I hear something go "clink" on the floor. I turn on the light and there on the floor was a penny. If I had taken one more step into the kitchen, the penny would have hit me on the head. That morning I'm telling my husband about the penny and I show it to him, a brand new 2005 shiny penny. We were both amazed that this had happened. How did it happen? I glanced over at the TV and there on the Today show, was the date, September 29, 2005. It was the date of my dear friend *Gloria's* birthday. I burst into tears. Gloria passed a while back and I just knew she had done this. BUT it gets better.

A couple of hours later I received a phone call. Three weeks earlier, I found a Yorkshire terrier wandering around and had fallen in love with him in the few hours I spent trying to find his owners. Fortunately, I was able to locate his owners and returned him. Well, the call I received that day was from the owners, they were working long hours and could no longer give him the attention he deserved and asked if I would take him. Of course, I said yes. He came into my home, took one look around, jumped on the couch (the same spot where Moo Cow always slept) let out a big sigh, and went to sleep. He had found his forever home. I KNOW Gloria was behind this. She helped me overcome the grief and pain from losing my Moo Cow. While Tucker cannot replace the "Moo Cow," he needed me as much as I needed him. I know Gloria was behind the messages of the country western party and the cow in the backyard that you received. We were inseparable in life and she's still with me in death.

Chapter Twelve

This Life Adventure Continues...

You see things; and you say, 'Why?' But I dream things
that never were; and I say, "Why not?"
George Bernard Shaw

I see the world as a spiritual Internet—with so much information out there that we can tap into, it's all about finding and connecting to the right site. Of course, the Spirits have to be "online" at the time, otherwise we get a blank screen. My beliefs have expanded: I've traveled down so-called paths of enlightenment, as well as veered off onto a couple of paths that no longer applied or were dead ends. I was raised Catholic, but when my religion didn't offer me answers to what I was experiencing, I realized I couldn't stay within the confines of only those beliefs. I had to expand and explore as far as my visions would take me.

For the most part, I consider my life normal, with some extraordinary blessings and critical spiritual lessons that needed to be experienced and now shared. I continue to experience many unusual incidents, often at unexpected moments. While working on a reading for a client, I'll often have psychic and/or physical events manifest themself. At such times it's important to acknowledge the Spirits with a "thank you" and to pay attention to what I feel they are revealing. Whether they turn on a light, send a scent or smell, whisper behind me, send feathers or pennies, move something, or even open a door, I try to see if there is a connection to the reading or if someone is stopping by for a surprise visit.

Then again, there was that time the door leading through the mudroom to the garage opened on its own, revealing a closed garage door. Considering that the mudroom door was locked, that was quite a feat. Once I heard footsteps, four to be exact, I grabbed my phone and ran out the front door and called the police on Spirit. The footsteps pretty much did it for me. Imagine trying to explain to the police officer the locked door just opened when the garage door was down. The policeman did notice the mudroom door was open all the way. The police dog found nothing. Was I surprised they couldn't find anyone in my house? Not at all. So I still have my chicken-medium moments, after all I'm human. And yes, I'm sure the other side had a good laugh out of that one. It seems Spirit has no problem sending their signs when needed. I'm not sure how many times I've tried to bend a spoon or make a pen move, but nothing happens. I guess having the ability to be an open channel should be enough, but it's not. I always want the other side to show me more, especially since I'm from Missouri, the Show-Me state. I want to be a psychic-medium sponge and soak it all up, never stop learning and seeing what new things can manifest. My fears may stop me for a couple of hours, but then I go right back searching for more.

All in all I am honored by Spirits' presence and give them constant thanks. Added to that, I know of no one who spontaneously speaks indigenous languages like myself to this extent, so I feel the need to always express the responsibility I whole-heartily accept. Throughout this journey I have gained some amazing insight. Hopefully my past can help your future.

***

By now, you realize from the many stories I've shared that our loved ones are often around us, whether to just check in and see what's going on in our lives or to lend love and support in their own way. They know our lives have been changed dramatically since they have left us, and a subtle reminder of their presence can go a long way. Please accept them and continue on with your own journey knowing they have been a blessed part of your life. It is the best gift you can give back, to keep on living and walking your own path. Losing a parent, partner or child doesn't change the fact you're still here and you need to continue to take steps, even tiny ones that may be extremely difficult to take to move forward. Remember that your life is vital to your soul's growth. Whatever your individual mission may be, it isn't over or you wouldn't be reading this book right now. No matter how painful a loss or your life situation, don't consider suicide an option. Not only does it stop you from continuing your soul's journey here, it changes the dynamics of those left around you and could hinder both your spiritual evolution and theirs. There have been a number of cases where I read families who have been victims to a loved one who commits an act of suicide. Often, a specific weighty energy is felt, it's not a bad energy, it just feels heavier to me. More regret than anything else seems to emerge, along with the sadness and pain they brought to the family and people they love. The best way to describe it is as if they are carrying a weight on their shoulders from their own personal act. This causes many issues I believe they still must deal with, something they will have to either learn to understand or revisit in order to move forward. Added to this is the extra burden they created by leaving loved ones lingering in guilt. So many of you say, "if only," or "what if?" and that only creates more personal pain. Allow yourself to release those thoughts and instead send healing and prayers to your loved one who made that choice. Understand it was their choice, based on their issues, not yours. When they do come to me in a vision, they often appear with others or with a health professional. This makes me believe they are receiving guidance with the issues they had here, possibly to help themselves see the world they were living in, and to help those left behind know they are being cared for in a healing environment. It's a comfort to know they are surrounded by loving beings. I would like to add that if you ever have personal issues or emotional residue from the loss of a loved one who chose suicide, there is nothing wrong with getting assistance. I recommend psychological counseling.

***

We all have a personal vision of life. As a child I didn't instantly know I was a psychic medium. The birth certificate didn't state I had mediumistic abilities when I arrived. Unfortunately I struggled with it, feared it, fought it tooth and nail, at times enjoyed it, only to push it aside thinking I was crazy a lot of the time. I assure you I didn't seek out something that's so controversial. It's simply who I am and the world I exist within. It took a while but I finally accepted it and the responsibilities that come with it.

I have learned to live by my own personal standards of integrity that have been molded and shaped through my abilities. Sharing these personal stories and exposing myself is a monumental step after a lifetime of hiding behind my telephone. I've never been one to say, "Hey! Look at me and what I can do!" Discussing my abilities has always been for family and a few close friends. I'm careful to share my visions with others, mainly because some may fear them and others don't believe. That being said, I wrote this book for those who do have an interest, and I believe it's important to get my message out to the public. Like peeping around the door that is cracked open, you get to experience my life. This whole new world emerges from another's point of view. Through my work, reading and testing, I've come to the conclusion that death is not the end of the line and more importantly, you have nothing to fear from it.

***

My firm belief is that other mediums should stand up and be tested. It's heartening to read about other mediums who are participating in experiments to test their abilities. They needed strength to step up to the plate, and they are willing to put themselves on the line to bring about change by providing evidence of their abilities. Hopefully, more universities will do research on mediums in the future. The more we explore, test and investigate, the more answers and validation we'll receive. I am proud to be one of the people who have been tested in a university setting. Instead of hiding, I chose to step up to the plate, fears included. Whether right or wrong, as Dr. Gary Schwartz states: "Let the data speak for itself." That is the bottom line. However, for me the human factor is as important as the data—being able to help others find a tiny bit of peace or help them take that next step in life without a loved one near. For many, mediums can show that their loved ones are around to offer comfort in their new life and for us to accept that same comfort in our new life. This can't replace them, but it can add a new depth to the phrase, "Spirits, they are present."

Think of your loved ones on the other side as an Internet connection. Some are clear, some speedy, others slow. No matter what type of connection you had, it still exists—even when a computer is turned off, the Internet is still there. It's the same with Spirit. When you learn how to co-exist with that connection, as in meditating or focusing, you can tune in and bring your connection/vibration up while they bring their connection/vibration down, thus meeting in the middle. I've spent my life learning to tune in and I'll continue to work at it. I'm always searching for a better connection. When loved ones come in, they don't come in on an ethereal level to me, they come in as if standing in the same room, looking right at me. At times, I go back to the way I was raised and occasionally look up at them. In those moments I get a sense they are waving their hands in front of me, to remind me to look straight ahead instead. I am not saying they are not in a location named Heaven, but I am saying they are in a state of Heaven which comes in many forms, according to your beliefs. They are closer than you realize, in a state of unimaginable beauty, which should give anyone comfort.

If you're having any psychic or mediumship experiences due to the loss of a loved one, savor them. If comfortable, reach out to someone you trust and share it with them. Also, be sure to give thanks, that's something you can give back to them.

You may also have personal "ah-ha!" psychic or mediumship moments, simply take note of them, accept it for what they are and begin to see where it can slowly lead you. One step at a time. Just because you have a couple of visions doesn't give you a new profession, it gives you insight to your life and those of loved ones beyond. When you walk slowly, you'll see and experience more than when you're running down the hill at full speed. Being a psychic and/or medium is the same—one step at a time. If you're trying to get to the end result too quickly, you'll find yourself getting nowhere fast. Also of importance is to mention and remind you that you're sure to come across those who will not believe that you received a message from a loved one or they won't believe you know something beforehand. That's okay. What you are given, is given to you because you can accept it, and may only be for you anyway. If you encounter others who come across negative, remind yourself, that it is their journey they chose to walk, not yours. If my ideas and experiences aren't fitting into someone else's "box" it doesn't mean I should disregard them. I believe in tolerance. Even when those past years weren't easy, what they have taught me made me a stronger person. Anyone who goes through a trauma has scars in one form or another, physical or mental. Yet they often say how they surprisingly came out stronger after such an experience. When I fell off a boat sideways and landed on a concrete dock, I was physically banged up with a broken elbow, bruised shoulder, hip and knee. Because it was physical everyone could accept the fact I was hurt and in discomfort so I had to slow down, let it heal with time and physical therapy. The same can be said for the Spiritual or an awakening psychic ability as well, even a spiritual crisis. When things come from all directions you can't charge through without taking stock, or you'll likely crash at some point. Step by step, find your focus. What do you want out of this? Join a group of like-minded people, talk it out, find a positive avenue. Learn from others and their experiences. You're already that much further ahead. I am thrilled to see all the books on the shelves and Internet these days, from self-help for Spiritual crisis, to learning how to meditate—reading personal accounts of spiritual leaders and learning about death and dying—there are so many incredible perspectives. They all give you avenues and choices to connect with new ideas that may resonate with you, so start now and pick another path later. I've read a variety of books where I'll take only three or four tidbits from each to help me see something in a new light. Then there were books that tell me the only way to meditate or receive information is to sit like a pretzel. It may work for some, however, I would end up with cramped and stiff legs. Sharing a number of my own tried and true ways may help you along the path you now find yourself walking. Finding ways to push the envelope helps us achieve greatness.

If this book gets a couple of you out there stirring and stimulated to move ahead through your pain, sadness, fearfulness and even to simply explore, then I've done what I set out to do. The spiritual possibilities are like the universe, endless. Do you think I knew as a child that someday I would be able to speak Yanomami? Of course not, why would I? It was never in my realm of possibilities or thoughts. You have also seen the journey I've taken and it hasn't been easy, but it also hasn't stopped me. When I was young, my grandparents used to say I was, "Little, but mighty." I would like to think that by the choices I made, they were right. I encourage you to exercise your options to be mighty in your pursuit of the spiritual. I'm not asking you to defy family, the law, or your personal beliefs. I am asking you to open yourself up for the possible and explore. Think of yourself as a colorful canvas, constantly adding new layers of paint to express even more of you. Days, weeks, or months go by and you add, change or completely repaint it, creating a new vibrant picture of yourself. So take your "abilities" and stretch them, expand them to see how far you can go. I'm hopeful someday soon to stretch and go all the way to South America to speak with the Yanomami people. This is a significant, yet enormous dream of mine with relevant content that could be revealed. I'm looking forward to completing this journey and standing face to face with the indigenous people while speaking their languages. After all, my tapes have been there, so why shouldn't I get to go? Considering that years ago I hadn't heard of them, shows you that anything is possible and often probable if you stick with it and believe. As soon as my documentary film crew shows up, I'm there!

***

I want to share some of the ways I learned how to connect with the other side through trial and error. I'm not saying this is a satisfaction-guaranteed way to meet your loved ones who have already passed to the other side. It's a way to go within yourself and connect on your own terms with your loved ones, or simply to gain some intuition. Who knows, maybe a spirit guide or angel might appear with a bit of wisdom. Of course it takes practice and patience, sometimes more than you think you have.

I found that there are so many ways to connect to your loved ones, whether you find it through your religion, your family, through music or meditation, self-help books, even classes, they are all ways that work, so try what feels right to you. Take that step and see where it leads. One small way I connect with loved ones residing on the other side is to close my eyes and open my hands, palms up, silently holding them out to the other side. Whenever I need a little lift, I ask them to take hold of them, just as when you need a little comfort here and someone holds your hand or helps you up—it's the same principle. I then slowly close my hands in order to hold in their precious energy they've sent. It's a little exercise you can do anywhere, anytime, day or night. When I open my palms once again, I feel a little more energized, and connected to my loved ones.

***

Many times while reading, which I find relaxing, I'll suddenly get information that seemingly comes from nowhere and I'll write it down hoping it makes sense at a later date. Surrounded by notes and scraps of paper with seemingly unimportant scribbles, I look at them as messages from Spirit with a dab of intuition. Scattered around, they lie on my desk and fill a number of files. Those that feel extremely strong seem to blast constantly within my mind, as if keeping me on alert. When this happens, time and patience are what allows the situation to unfold. Do you ever read a word and then immediately hear it on the TV or radio, maybe even hear someone say it at the exact time you read it? Many claim this as coincidence, but I don't believe in coincidences. I believe that such occurrences always hold a purpose, a situation or a reminder. What better way to gain attention than to double the experience or thought? Next time you encounter a so-called coincidence, see what it is telling you or paralleling in your life. If you stop and pay attention, you may be surprised.

Music often takes hold of me and connects me to my intuition and to the other side as well. I can be singing and some tiny little piece of information slips through and suddenly I realize it has importance. While walking through the house one day I suddenly started singing, "Mama Mia" by Abba. Since that song seldom comes to mind, I stopped and thought to myself, "Why is this song suddenly coming through seemingly out of nowhere?" I decided to turn on the TV since the musical had been on HBO months ago, just to see if it might be playing again. Sure enough, it was going to start in the next half hour. Since I wanted to DVR it and missed my opportunities in the past, I now was given a chance. High five to Spirit!

Waking up one morning I realized I was humming a song and then sang one line. Carl was already awake and he said, "Your right!" Shaking the grogginess off, it took me a minute to understand what he was saying. Then it hit me, I realized I was right. I was singing only one line by Paul Simon's song, "Mother and Child Reunion" and that was, "A mother and child reunion is only a motion away." Now, no matter what the song actually signifies has nothing to do with what I personally took from it. I smiled when realizing what I was singing upon awakening because it directly related to that day. It was Mother's Day and my son was coming home from college to see me, which made it an extremely wonderful mother and child reunion. I smiled all day long.

Many people, myself included, believe music is very healing. It also can help you in becoming more sensitive to receiving intuitive and psychic information. Whether listening to soft flute music, chants or sometimes rock music, they all put me in different meditative moods. Of course some days I can't handle any music and just want peace and quiet. If you're just starting out, I would suggest a quiet setting, then work your way up to a little soft music. There are even times I meditate with the TV buzzing in the background. It's really all about personal preference and what you feel most comfortable with when trying to become more open. I've always enjoyed occasions when thinking of someone special and having their favorite song come on the radio. I take that as a sign they are letting me know they are around. My choice in music is often a reflection of what is to come in my future readings. Paying attention to a certain mood or feeling from Spirit usually diverts me in a direction that I need to travel.

Next time you're thinking of someone and a song emerges that you haven't thought about in years and years, take it as a sign, you may be receiving a hello from your deceased loved one who's been gone for a while.

There are days when information hits me like a ton of bricks that just fell out of the sky. Then there are days when information comes through that makes no sense at all, but it just can't be ignored. Who would have imagined that seeing butter, then Parkay, would mean someone on the other side wanted to tell me they know someone who lived in "Land O'Lakes"? I have learned to listen to what I receive. I don't so much consider myself on the clock 24/7, but when I get a certain feeling I know to remain aware. For you it may take time and practice to learn what something means to you. So, if you suddenly picture a car accident in your mind don't immediately freak out, simply be more cautious when driving. I always try to use logic first, especially whenever something extremely strong comes through. Freaking out will only make any situation worse. Believe me, because I have been there so many times in the past, I can definitely say I've learned from experience, so learn from mine. Don't suddenly see or feel something and then throw caution to the wind thinking it's ridiculous. The wind just may come back as a tornado.

Asking for a sign is a wonderful way to connect with deceased loved ones. Keep in mind if you don't get one, don't think they aren't there or don't love you. You could be missing the sign. I enjoy talking with them, such as asking a loved one to help watch over me on an upcoming trip. I even ask them to help find spirits for me on the other side. However, I don't try to constantly contact them with everyday issues, unless of course I lost my cell phone. My advice is to ask, accept, and always give thanks.

I thought a little exercise might get you moving in the right direction, or at least make you realize that it's possible to actually make a connection on your own. We're not asking for the lottery here, folks. We're asking for a simple connection to Spirit in some form. Since I already believe we are spirit forms in a human bodysuit, I believe it's not such a stretch to possibly connect with the spirit world.

Let's try this:

Sit down, get comfortable—there's no need to be dressed up, so wear something comfortable and loose. Have a pad of paper and your favorite pen or pencil nearby. Whether sitting on a chair, lying on the floor or a couch, just be comfortable. Now start by saying a simple little prayer or positive affirmation, and have it come from the heart. If you don't want to say a prayer or affirmation, then read something inspirational that is simple and not too long. I always begin by asking for "protection of the white universal light." I ask for it to surround and protect me. Now close your eyes and take a couple of deep slow breaths—three to six will do. Visualize that you're walking down a road. This road can be anywhere. It may be a gravel country road, a highway, a road through the universe if you want—create whatever feels right.

As you begin to walk down this road, you hear the sound of your footsteps as they peacefully drum down the path. What do you see or feel or hear? Anything? Nothing? Stop for a moment and take it in. Look around. Anything unusual? Now, open your eyes and write down what you just experienced. Did you see something but not hear anything? Did you hear something or someone, but didn't see them? Maybe you felt something? Write down only what you perceived. Take a deep breath slowly. Okay, you're now done for the day. Give thanks for whatever you received. Wow, that took all of maybe 5 minutes! Okay, now put your work aside, and date it. Take a deep breath, get up and go on with your day and have a nice one at that.

A day passes, maybe three or four, and you have time to do this exercise again. You can choose the same place or try a new place, a chair, the floor, whatever. Once again bring your pad of paper and pen. If possible try to commit to this exercise at least once a week. Then maybe work your way up to twice a week and see what happens.

Okay, begin again by saying your prayer, affirmation or inspirational reading. You surround yourself in a protective universal light, then draw in a couple slow deep breaths and release them. As you close your eyes, you begin to walk down the road again. Is it the same? Different? What road appears to you today? Don't think in advance, let it come to you. Keep walking. Look around, anything interesting emerge? Just enjoy the moment. Now, slowly open your eyes and write what emerged this time around. Did you just remember you need bread at the grocery store, or you have to pick up the kids at 4:00 and take them to hockey practice? Maybe you need to change the second paragraph in the proposal you're writing for work? Any number of things that filter through your mind are okay to see during this meditation. Write it down, it must be important. Okay, you're finished for today! Give thanks. Boy, that was easy, easy, easy. Don't forget to take your list to the grocery store!

Now, the next time you try this, I want you to start clearing your mind before you get started. Get your pad of paper and write down the things you think you need to do or finish that day. Once completed, say your prayer, affirmation or inspirational saying, close your eyes, surround yourself in white protective universal light, take a couple of slow, deep breaths and start walking down the road. This time you still may have a mental grocery list going, but you're also clearer. You suddenly see something different. Quick flashes of little scenarios pop up on the road before you. It could be anything: A new car, someone at work who is pregnant that you didn't know about, a piece of mail in the mailbox that comes across extremely important and so on. When you finish, sure you may have added a couple of things to the grocery list or the job you have to execute later this week, but you also saw something new and where the heck did that come from? Write it down and date it.

I would like to urge you to give this a try for a couple of weeks or months. If you want to do this every day fine, or if you want to try it once a week, fine. I do feel that the more you do this simple meditation, the more it becomes integrated as a daily or weekly routine. But let's take it one moment at a time.

Let's assume you've been doing this for a couple of weeks or months and you decide to see if Grandma Eleanor who died many years past has anything to say or show you. Let's walk the road again, and invite Grandma Eleanor to walk with you. You don't have to see or hear her—let's just assume she is there, walking with you. You've been walking for a while and you sort of forgot Grandma was next to you because you're walking down the road to see what's up ahead. Suddenly a little piece of information pops up, possibly a memory from the past, maybe a feeling or a scent you relate to Grandma, like her homemade pies or a fancy perfume—she might even have whispered something. Whatever you get, accept it with gratitude and then thank her for taking a walk with you. When you open your eyes write down what you received. Don't try to find something that isn't there, let it come to you. If you don't get anything this time, there is always next time. I know that will be difficult, but you'll begin to understand that the more you simply open up to what they wish to share, the easier it will become. Don't project, simply allow.

You may also receive a light tap on the shoulder or cheek from a "friend." If you're not ready for something like this to happen, then gently ask them to wait until you're ready. I remember the first time I was brushed by Spirit, it was the lightest of touches yet it felt like I had just been knocked over. I was so surprised, I'm sure my response was comical to the other side. It still doesn't stop me from doing what I love and they know that. I guess that's why they put up with me!

This is just one simple example to help you easily learn to meditate. You can choose to follow it or find your own way. Just always remember your intention and purpose.

After a couple of months I would like you to look back over your notes and the dates and see if any of it matches what has happened in your everyday life. Did you find out a co-worker was pregnant? Gosh, you knew that! You got a new car? Wasn't expecting that but it happened in the most unusual way, and you knew that too. Did you see something else you didn't know about? Keep in mind, this is just a simple little exercise. It's to allow you to open and stretch your mind to what is possible out there for the taking. Be sure to keep track of your notes and always date them. It will offer you validation for the future.

Another little exercise I would like to share is a dream exercise:

I often found that when the languages spontaneously come through during the day, I dream more vividly at night. This is a great tool because it helps inform me as to what I will see or need to see coming up in my daily life. Since I often look at my dreams for personal clues, my belief is that they also bring guidance for my readings. I consider this a fringe benefit. I try to encompass the many facets of my abilities to help others. When I start dreaming vividly I believe this happens so I'm able to connect it with a situation I'm currently in at that time or need to deal with in the future.

One such dream came to me about Ipupiara, the man who has helped me translate my tapes. I've had email correspondence with him on and off over the years, but never have had the opportunity to actually meet him. I was hopeful that day would come. He has given me so much by having my tapes translated that I wanted to thank him someday in person for being a connection from the Spirit world to ours. It was while I was going through a series of dreams about him that an extraordinary event happened.

I received an email from a man who happened across my website and saw the name Ipupiara. He has been friends with him for years and had even heard Ipupiara speak about me and wondered why we never met. I emailed him back that with Ipupiara's schedule, as well as mine, it just never seemed to work with him traveling so much. He emailed that he and Ipupiara were going to be in Long Island in June. If I was available, we could finally meet.

The dates not only worked out but they were close to the dates we were actually planning to be there, which was amazing in itself, so we made a slight adjustment to our schedule and I suddenly found that one of my long time wishes was going to happen. I was going to meet Ipupiara.

When the date finally arrived I was extremely excited, and a bit nervous. We were to meet at the home where Ipupiara was staying. His host and hostess were generous for allowing our meeting to take place there. I was extremely grateful to them as well as Ipupiara's friend Larry, who made this happen. It was a living dream come true. It was during that visit that I found I was speaking a fourth language, Canamari. I was thankful for paying attention to my dreams so when the opportunity presented itself, I was already aware something was going to take place.

Dreams can be confusing and long and have crazy twists and turns in them. One thing I have learned to do is when I first wake up, I try to remember my dreams backwards. Yes, backwards. It sounds sort of backwards, but it actually really works. Trying to remember the beginning can make you forget the end. Starting at the end makes you think of what happened before that and before that. Writing it down helps as well, although I'll be the first to admit I don't always write them down, especially if I wake up at 3:00 a.m. I'm just not disciplined with my dreams. However, I do listen to them and appreciate their worth, especially when I feel strongly about one.

If you wish to know more about dreams, please go to your local book store and take your pick. Knowledge is power and dreams hold knowledge. I have a nice little library of dream books to help me when stuck, but I always rely on my own interpretations first.

Another transition I have had to deal with and accept over time is seeing faces at night when I close my eyes. This started in my twenties and increased in my late thirties. I would usually go to sleep and lay on my right side. It would only take minutes before faces would begin to appear one after another. It would start from about three feet out and slowly the faces would move toward my face. They were usually in a bluish white glow, yet on occasion I would see them in almost full color. As they slowly moved in closer, one after another, the faces would get not so much distorted, but the shifting or the movement caused them to alter a little back and forth. It took about ten seconds from when I first saw the face to the time it closed in. The face would get so close—I would usually jerk back and cry out as it moved through my own face and beyond. Then there are times it would happen so fast I couldn't react. It never failed, the times that I did jerk back, Carl would always say, "The faces?" to which I would reply, "Ya." This often nightly event I haven't quite figured out as of yet. They don't seem to be familiar people, but sometimes I'll see the same ones. Whether they are some type of guide, angelic being, past relative or they're for a future client, I don't know for sure. I have had the fortunate or unfortunate privilege of feeling the coolness as they pass through me on occasion, and that's when I usually immediately turn over to my left side.

***

If you're having any experiences, group support with like-minded individuals who want to learn and grow in their psychic and medium abilities could be vital to you. This way you provide guidance for each other as well as having someone around as you start emerging from your shell. I did this for many years. I was part of an Association for Research & Enlightenment group that met weekly. We read from the book provided, meditated and then had a discussion session.

The Forever Family Foundation is a great organization to get involved with, especially if you lost a loved one. They understand the need to connect with like minds and explore at the same time. As their website indicates, they were created to help further the understanding of Afterlife Science through research and education while providing support and healing for people in grief.

It is an honor and privilege to be on the Medium Advisory Board, as well as a certified medium with the Forever Family Foundation.

***

One last exercise you may want to try that is introspective and simple is meditating on a word. Whether it's a person's name, or a word such as Spirit, Love, Forgiveness or Kindness, just pick a word that feels good to you. Say your prayer, affirmation or inspirational saying and surround yourself in the white protective universal light. Ask what you need to understand about this word and then write it down.

Let's say you wish to dedicate this meditation to Mike. You decided to pick his name because you're having a problem at work with Mike and you're stuck. Everyone thinks he's the greatest thing since sliced bread and you just don't see it. He may be a diligent worker, but he's also an ass around you. Ask Spirit to please show you some avenues you can take to be more in harmony with Mike and then see what happens. You may find some very simple suggestions that you never thought of because you were blocked emotionally from seeing them. Stay open-minded throughout this process. When you're finished writing these suggestions down, give thanks and end your session. You'll usually gather some easy solutions to help the situation as well as feel more peaceful toward Mike. It's a win-win situation. Let me know how it goes.

The Shake-up

I was asked to be on an evening Internet radio show hosted by Forever Family Foundation in September 2009. This would be the first time I would be doing readings in a quick succession via an Internet show. Each reading would last only minutes, so I knew I had to relay the messages quickly as well as have them be validating. I admit my energy level was at a high point. A meditation that afternoon showed me many Spirits and pieces of information already, even though whomever was going to call in was a big question mark. Trust the process, I always remind myself, and so I did. I was going to be working in tandem with another medium during the show, which was helpful to give me time to regroup after each call. Spirit works in amazing ways. It's interesting to find out, by a throw of the universal dice, who ends up on the other line and yet I already had information come through for them that afternoon, maybe before they even knew they were going to call.

The evening was a success and almost all of the information I received that afternoon had been validated. With the show over there was still an extreme amount of energy that radiated around me and through me. It was as if the Spirit world wasn't through with me just yet.

As I hung up the phone, it was time to head to the kitchen for some chamomile tea to help me relax. While sitting in my comfy chair I drank the tea and tried to calm down but still felt extremely energetic—that's when I decided I needed to do a couple chores. I figured I might as well use up some of this energy rolling through me. When finished, I decided to head for bed. I completed my nightly routine and got into bed next to my husband and kissed him goodnight. I snuggled under the covers and got comfortable. While lying on my side, facing away from Carl, I realized after a couple of minutes the bed was shaking. I turned toward Carl saying, "Quit shaking the bed," wondering, *What is he doing?"*

He turned toward me saying, "I'm not shaking the bed, I thought you were shaking the bed!"

We both sat up and realized the bed was still shaking! Carl said, "I think we're having an earthquake."

I responded as I glanced around, "Nothing else in the room is shaking, but the bed!"

It almost felt like it was vibrating and for the record we don't have the kind of bed that takes quarters! Suddenly, as quickly as it started, it stopped. Carl leaned over, kissed me and rolled over and went to sleep. I however, laid back down knowing this wasn't normal, but I would check the U.S. Geological Survey (USGS) online in the morning just to make sure. A couple of minutes passed and it happened again. The bed began to shake lightly almost like a vibration of some sort and this time I felt someone lightly grab my legs above my ankles and hold them gently. I slowly glanced up to see if someone was at the end of the bed and even though my legs were under the covers, I still looked. Nothing. Someone was holding my legs tenderly and I couldn't see them. The bed continued to shake and I looked over and heard Carl snoring next to me. *Great, now what?* As I tried not to be afraid, I asked this Spirit to let go of my legs and they did. The bed stopped shaking as well. Oddly enough I almost felt more relaxed, as if this spiritual being were releasing some of the energy that I had stored up from earlier in the evening while doing the show. I laid there thinking how strange this was and wondered if it would happen again. Sure enough about ten minutes later it started up again. The bed began to vibrate but this time no one grabbed my legs. I lay there in awe thinking no one would believe me if I shared this story with them. The following morning I asked Carl if he remembered the bed shaking and he looked at me and said, "Yeah, of course. Why?"

"Because it happened two more times after you fell asleep and someone grabbed my legs the second time!" I replied.

"And you didn't scream?" He asked.

"No," I said. "It was really odd, but not frightening. It was almost as if someone was calming me down."

I did get online that morning to the USGS website to check for earthquakes in my area and there weren't any of any size the night before or even that morning.

I was curious if it would happen the following month since I was doing the Internet show again. It didn't. Whether I had learned to let go of that extra energy after the show or whether it was a different group of spirits, I don't know. I do feel whoever was there was trying to help me relax. I realized I had come a long way from years past, for it had actually calmed me down instead of frightening me.

January of the following year I encountered another shake up. I was diagnosed with ovarian cancer. It was an extremely emotional time. I didn't see it coming on any level, even though I'm psychic, so again I was reminded I can't change some things. I had been following the progress of a small cyst on my ovary, but as we all know cysts are not usually cancerous and this one was no exception. There weren't any signs that were flashing a warning this could be cancer—nobody on the other side told me either. As I came to find out after the fact, ovarian cancer had very basic symptoms: bloating, a feeling of fullness, gas, frequent or urgent urination, nausea, indigestion, constipation, diarrhea, menstrual disorders such as vaginal bleeding, pain during intercourse, fatigue, backaches. All these are signs and you don't need to have all of them. Most of us have some of them on any given day. Sure I had bloating, and had been constipated at times, didn't most women? I actually had very few signs but they ended up being signs nonetheless. I went in for surgery to have the cyst removed and possibly a salpingo-oophorectomy (removal of the fallopian tube and ovary) if needed. I could have elected to wait a couple more months if I wanted to see if the cyst would change—however it was staying about the same and I was starting to have some pain in the abdominal area. This was the deciding factor when added to a couple of other issues I was having. I was working out four times a week and would often have spot bleeding afterward. The gynecologist agreed this wasn't normal, and thought it could be from the cyst. I went back and forth for checkups for four months and realized this wasn't getting any better, so why not have it taken care of. The surgery went extremely well even though a salpingo-oophorectomy was needed—I was happy to just have this taken care of and now I could get on with my life. When I went in the following week to be given a clean bill of health, instead I heard words I never thought to hear. "Janet, you have ovarian cancer." I never realized how different life becomes after those few words are thrown at you. Suddenly the ground you're standing on gives a little, uncertainty sets in. My next step was a second surgery within the week to have a total hysterectomy and to make sure the cancer hadn't spread to other areas. Although it was confined and my prognosis looked good, there was also the possibly I may need chemotherapy. Within seconds, my life had changed. I went through so many emotions in the days to follow and found the one I liked the most was to stay positive. I made sure that I was positive and kept a strong voice whenever I spoke with anyone. In my quiet moments I wondered where this would lead me, and reminded myself I would be strong and conquer this like many other cancer survivors have. Then, there were moments when I cried. Having to call my son who was at college hundreds of miles away was the most difficult. I was upbeat and even cheery until I heard his voice crack and a quiet sob, then I lost it. I knew at times life sucks, and at this moment, it did. After our cry, I again, "got positive" and so did he.

The following week I went in for surgery a second time. A total hysterectomy was performed and biopsies had been taken from the abdomen down. The gynecologist stated everything looked good, but we would see what the pathology report came back with. Within four days I received a call telling me everything was clean and they found no more cancer. Even better was the fact that I would not need chemotherapy since I was considered Stage I. I was told by the doctor I was a miracle and this was a miracle because they don't usually find too many cases of Stage I ovarian cancer. And that is why I am including this story. I want more women to have miracles too. If this touches even one woman and you think you have some of the symptoms, please know your body and follow up on it. If I had chosen to wait, my outcome would have been different. Being a cancer survivor has changed my life and shown me blessings in so many new ways. It has made me, or rather reminded me, to do what I need to do, and do it now.

It was the day before my second surgery that the Haiti earthquake hit. Over the next couple days while recovering I watched what scenes played out before me on the news. After recovering from two surgeries, I was out of commission for a while and so I did lots of reading and relaxing. So it was a surprise when I went to bed one evening and my bed began to shake again. It was a subtle vibration, but enough to wake me up. I wondered if this time it was an earthquake. Looking around, nothing else was shaking. I wondered who was trying to get a message across. I found out.

The following morning, I turned on the TV and saw that Chile had an earthquake while I had been sleeping. Since then, my bed has shaken when there was a mine explosion in West Virginia, an earthquake in China and again when a mine exploded in Russia. Each time, I have felt it the night before. Carl has felt some of them, but not all. We have come to accept that the only thing we can do is send positive healing prayers, blessings, and peace to the families and the planet.

Life continued and I believed I was pretty much on track for what I was working toward when a new adventure popped into my life. Waking up and walking into the bathroom, it's common for me to glance in the mirror and see my famously wild bed head. Because my hair is naturally curly it has a habit and mind of its own during the night hours. So when I smiled at the mirror, thankful no one could see my morning hair, I noticed something a bit different: my neck looked bigger to me. Was it my imagination or something more? Was I getting fatter and it became obvious? Or was my neck that large all along and I never realized it? After a couple of weeks of continued surveillance and after one of my sisters noticed it as well, I made an appointment with the endocrinologist.

Weeks later I was told my thyroid needed to be removed. It was shot and now expanding to a second double chin. I was ready for it to be removed and to move on with life. The week after surgery, sitting in the surgeon's office for a post check-up, I was informed I had thyroid cancer. This darn cancer thing happened again. Well, hell, if that didn't suck. The radioiodine treatment was planned, known as the "big drink." All my life I have heard comments of how "easy" thyroid cancer is—well, I disagree. What they easily gloss over is, the diet required, the shots, the "big drink" and the emotion of the prognosis. Since this is my forum I'm here to tell you, thyroid cancer isn't always easy and if you say it to my face, you're going to get an earful! I tried to joke about it with the fact I couldn't have ice cream or chocolate at my disposal on this diet, not that I ate it every day, it was a just-in-case scenario. Or maybe it was that I was told I had cancer twice in eight months that made me more introspective. Whatever the case, I learned this time around, a positive attitude was not only a good thing to have, it was required. No one is exempt from cancer, so be compassionate to all those who suffer from it no matter what type they have or what stage they are in.

Nothing like a shot in the butt to keep you in the moment—ok, maybe it was closer to the hip area, but still it's awakening. Two days and two shots later, then the following day it was time for the "big drink" as it was referred to by the Nuclear Medicine Physician. The big drink actually was quite small and almost tasteless in a warm-drinking-fountain-kind-of-way. As simple as this may have seemed, the emotion of knowing I was drinking something nobody would touch was huge. A week later the scan was taken and I was given a good prognosis. The radiation was killing the remaining cancerous thyroid tissue. The following days and months have been filled with appointments I don't want, but are a necessary precaution so I don't have to hear another doctor tell me I have cancer yet again.

The cancer experience seemed to make me stronger—as I discovered in the months ahead. It was Christmas, and a wonderful party brought the entire family together for a grand display of food, drink, laughter, and boundless generosity. To top off the joyous holiday, my sisters, their families, and my Mom left for Las Vegas the following afternoon to celebrate my niece's belated 21st birthday. Because my son was 20, we decided to wait a year to make the famous family voyage out to the luminous desert oasis. I had no doubt that my Mom and sisters would not be opposed to a second journey and another shot to win big. For the record, I have no advantage over anyone else in Las Vegas, but I still like to imagine the headline "Psychic Hits Jackpot." The mini-vacation had come to an end, and after checking out of the hotel my sisters noticed that my Mom was not at their previously decided meeting spot in the Bellagio lobby. It was obvious to them that she got an early start on the day to get in some last-minute gambling. After all, she did win a couple hundred dollars before heading to bed the night before. They searched the casino but to no avail, and the unanswered calls to her cell phone and room caused anxiety to flood their souls like a breach of the Hoover Dam. Security and maintenance arrived only to get no answer at her door. Upon entry, the worst was confirmed—Mom had passed in her sleep. The shock and pain of a great loss resonates within each of us, and I am no exception. I searched for signs I may have missed but realized it no longer mattered what I got, it was her time and her place to go. And looking back, she did a fine job choosing where and how she passed. She checked out in style, from one beautiful, classy place filled with positive energy and a beautiful view to the next. What a blessing, a nearly perfect way for my Mom to go. In the days since I've asked Mom to give me some signs that she is doing well. After all, she knew I could still communicate with her, but I worried, "Would my emotions get in the way?" On the morning of her wake, my sadness woke me up early and I asked for a sign to quell my grief. Only moments later, the radio alarm clock went off and the music began to play the song, "Only the Good Die Young." I just stared at the clock, eyes swollen and jaw open. She knew! She had read my manuscript and she knew this was one of the few significant songs I mentioned. I thanked her with a smile, though it hardly slowed the tears. The following morning, the radio alarm clock went off at the same time. As if Billy Joel's song weren't enough, my mom retained her generosity and played another song for me. Paul Simon's "Mother and Child Reunion" played seemingly louder than normal. I began to cry. I knew she was letting me know, that in the whole scheme of life, it is really only a short time before we will be together again. Until then, I wait for more signs from any and all generous spirits.

My Life, My Thanks

I look back over all the stories and realize I have walked quite a journey and there is more to come. Traveling through a number of stories left me crying, laughing and in awe. I hope you've enjoyed reading about my experiences, better yet I hope you learned something in the process that you can implement in your life. These experiences that have happened along the way were often frightening, but personal drive has pushed me through those fears. I had some tough lessons to learn. Many were exhilarating and I'm blessed to have been a part of them, large or small. It would be wrong to say I'm always right in my readings and what I perceive as correct. There are times I am wrong and I freely admit it. No one is perfect. Through it all I have learned some semblance of balance between the physical and the spiritual. I have been honored to speak the languages of indigenous tribes for over 16 years now. I have high hopes that one day I will have the opportunity to visit and speak with them and report back my experiences. Is this the ultimate proof of reincarnation, the ultimate proof of channeling the spirit world, or both or neither? This is just another road I know I will travel when the time is right. We will have to see what lies ahead. In the meantime I'll get my hiking shoes ready.

Speaking with Spirits who have passed on is an honor and I have been blessed to meet so many sacred beings along the way. I'm honored I am a vessel for their messages. I wake up each day wondering where I'll be lead to next. What steps will I take to further create my future of hope and healing for others, as well as for myself? I am constantly in transition like everyone who walks this planet. And yes, it's a joy to be here to explore.

I hope my work will encourage more mediums to be tested so more scientific experiments can be created. This may aid others to see what exists beyond the five senses. Life is so miraculous.

I don't take my abilities lightly, it is a responsibility that weighs heavily at times, yet can offer so much healing and peace.

I hope this book gives you an idea of who I am and the path I have chosen to walk. At times I felt I've been pushed on this path, other times have fallen and crash-landed on the solid ground below, not to mention the times that prayer has carried me to the next point.

I have learned that no matter what your belief system is, there is always room to expand it. Honor one another and where each comes from and the beliefs they hold. Don't judge a nation by a few.

Hopefully, after reading my book, you will consider the afterlife plausible, although, I know rationally that may not happen.

I do hope it will at least open your eyes to what is possible and the opportunities you hold within your mind. You never know what your potential is, so be open, be ready.

And last, cherish those you love. No matter what age they are or circumstance they are in.

A simple hello, a hug, a kiss or a phone call can mean so much.

Remember you are here for a reason, find it, live it and love it to the best of your ability. Doing this out of love for what is and what can be is why I have chosen to share my story. I hope you have felt it though my words and please know: *Spirits…They Are Present.*

With Many Blessings!

SHUNGO

Acknowledgements

I have been blessed by so many people who have crossed my path in this life. Many of them I have known for years and some are newcomers. Over time I have come to realize that life is certainly an ever-changing canvas on which we paint our thoughts and actions. I would like to specifically thank the following people for being the vibrant colors of my life mural:

To my Husband, Carl—I appreciate your support, love and patience. You have gone from skeptic to believer; this gives me hope for mankind! Thank you for your strong shoulders to lean on through all my exploratory and unfathomable experiences.

To my Son, Matt—You have been such a wonderful presence in my life. May you find wisdom and joy in all things It is a blessing and honor to be your "Momsa." Keep your creative spirit always, love ya kid!

Debbie Bandle—You above all others understand the journey I have walked. Your support has been phenomenal and I thank you for holding my hand through the path I've chosen. You've been a wonderful big sister. My gratitude always.

Mom—Your love has been a blessing and a prized treasure. The unwavering faith you've always had in me has allowed my journey to expand to new heights. Thanks for accepting who I need to be. *(I am blessed that my Mom was able to read my manuscript and her acknowledgement before she passed. In honor of her memory, I decided to keep this acknowledgement as is.)*

Dad—The inquisitive nature you passed down and the many challenges you placed before me helped create and bring insight to who I am today. Thanks for the push.

Hermina— Many would claim fear in telling their Mother-in-law they are a psychic medium. I wasn't one of them. Thanks for your support, but more importantly for all the wonderful Sunday dinners!

Phran and Bob Ginsberg—Two amazing people with so much compassion. I am privileged to have met you both, and blessed by our friendship. Your mission to bring research, education, support and healing is a gift to us all.

Dianne Arcangel—You have been a sounding board that always comes back with wonderful advice and spell check. Our chats have been "amazing." Thank goodness for the Internet, but more so for our friendship!

Dr. Lou Marincovich, Ph.D.—I would like to thank you for your assistance in editing my manuscript. You have been a joy to work with and as our paths became synchronized by the universe, a truly wonderful blessing to me.

Gary Schwartz Ph.D.—I appreciate your open-mindedness and for standing on the cliff of possibilities. The Susy experiment has continued to have a profound impact.

Julie Beischel Ph.D.—The professional and caring nature you portray shows that quality and accurate testing of mediumship is in good hands. Thanks for being there bridging the gap.

John Perkins—I will always be extremely grateful for the path you chose which crossed mine. Thank you for answering that first email. It was life changing.

In Memory of Bernardo Peixoto—Ipupiara-My friend Ipu-You added more depth to my life than you can imagine. Your gifts and abilities were truly from beyond. I thank you for being the wisdom keeper of my words and for the gift of helping me share them.

I offer many thanks to my generous clients for their stories they have allowed me to use. It's a privilege and blessing to share your words. My gratitude to:

Mike Boyd, William Kaspari, Carol & Roland, Kristen, Colleen Walski, Christine, Sherry, Jackie Hummert, Valerie Tatalias, Lou Marincovich Ph.D., Angie & Greg Key, and to Mike & Lori Buehler for their story that mirrored my son's.

Gratitude to Clare and Sherry for—The wake-up call.

Teri Watkins at AuthorHouse-It has been a pleasure to work with you throughout the publishing process. Your calming voice, knowledge and time has been a blessing. I would like to think the Spirits hand-picked exactly what I needed.

To all my family, friends and clients not mentioned above—Thank you for touching my life and adding the many vibrant colors that make me who I am. As a wise man once said to me,

"Shungo"

This means:

From My Heart to Yours!

Transcendental Spirits, Guides and Shamans who have come into my life—Thank you for showing me that Spirit lives on.

And to you, my dear reader, whether—On the other side, up, beyond, through the tunnel or wherever you choose to believe they exist, just know, *Spirits…They Are Present.*

I know of no more encouraging fact than the unquestioned
ability of a man to elevate his life by conscious endeavor.
Henry David Thoreau

Janet Mayer
P.O. Box 510426
St. Louis, MO 63151
www.JanetMayer.net

Websites you may find of interest and useful:
(Current upon publication of this book)

Forever Family Foundation
www.foreverfamilyfoundation.org

Afterlife Encounters
www.afterlife-encounters.com

Edgar Cayce (A.R.E.)
www.edgarcayce.org

Dream Change
www.dreamchange.org

www.Kimberlyboydlegacy.org

A tribute to Scott
www.ScottHelpingChildren.com
www.ScottWalski.com

CdLS Foundation
www.CdLS.org

Maggie Moo Cards
www.maggiemoocards.etsy.com

www.gotboatgear.com

Holotropic Breathwork™
www.Holotropic.com

Made in the USA
Las Vegas, NV
06 January 2025

15942587R00132